A BROAD VISION

PETER PUGH

A BROAD VISION

The Price Bailey Story

Published in the UK in 2013 by
Company Histories Ltd
Saltingsgarth
Broad Lane
Brancaster
Norfolk
PE31 8AU

ISBN: 978-184831-668-3

Typeset in Classical Garamond
by Marie Doherty

Printed in Europe by Latitude Press

Contents

Foreword

The origins of Price Bailey can be traced back some 75 years, when Leslie Benten as L.H. Benten & Co. set up at 6 High Street, Bishop's Stortford. Within a few years, Stanley Price and Reg Bailey were recruited and it was these two chartered accountants who took the firm forward after Leslie Benten left in the early 1950s.

While the Bishop's Stortford office remained the centre of Price Bailey, the firm expanded throughout East Anglia over the next 50 years. Stanley Price and Reg Bailey were shrewd managers and recruited skilful and personable accountants who gave the firm a fully justified reputation for reliable service by people who were always a pleasure to deal with.

The Bishop's Stortford office benefited from the expansion of the nearby Stansted Airport and the Cambridge office from the Cambridge Phenomenon which began in the 1960s and continued to grow and attract many successful technology companies.

The British economy has grown since the end of the Second World War but there have been a number of recessions. Price Bailey has weathered those recessions and has continued to grow. At the beginning of the twenty-first century the current Executive Chairman, Peter Gillman, succeeded John Riseborough as Senior Partner and began a process of departmentalising the firm, a process which everyone now agrees has been crucial in enabling Price Bailey to grow even faster in the last ten years.

Price Bailey expanded out of its East Anglian comfort zone in 2007 when it opened an office in the City of London and in 2011 it acquired a firm in Mayfair in the West End. Between these two important developments it also acquired a practice in Guernsey. And the professionalism of the firm has not gone unnoticed with it being named 'Large Firm of the Year' in the *Accountancy Age* awards in 2010.

In an age when businesses come and go within a few years, it's encouraging to think that a professional firm can prosper and grow, without losing sight of its history and character.

All of us, whether working for the firm or living locally here in Bishop's Stortford, would like to wish everyone at Price Bailey, now and in the past, our congratulations on reaching this milestone.

Mark Prisk, MP for Hertford and Stortford, Minister for Housing and formerly Minister for Business, Innovation and Skills

The early partners, Stanley Price and Reginald Bailey.

Introduction

This is a book about the 75 years of a very successful accountancy practice.

They are 75 important years both in the history of the United Kingdom, encompassing the Second World War and all the recessions and periods of growth in the 60-year period following that war, and in the history of accountancy and how it has had to adapt to the changes in both accounting practices and accounting technology.

As you will see, the Price Bailey story is one of growth from a single partner in one office to 22 partners in seven offices, not only in East Anglia but in the City and West End of London as well as in Guernsey in the Channel Islands. Price Bailey, which became a Limited Liability Partnership in 2004, is now the 29th biggest accountancy practice in the country. Its new Managing Director, Martin Clapson, is also Chairman of the European Board of the International Association of Professional Accountants (IAPA).

Many people view accountants as a necessary adjunct to their life because the law of the land demands that financial dealings, whether personal or corporate, be properly assessed and recorded and that the correct tax, if any is due, be paid. There is no doubt that Price Bailey has always been meticulous in making sure this work is done properly and in due time.

However, it has also always been the practice of the firm to carry out the above in an open and friendly manner and to offer more than the mere adding up of sums. As Richard Price, son of one of the original partners and a very long-serving member of Price Bailey, will tell you in the book, the firm has always made sure that they were close to the clients and often mixed with them socially.

As you will also see, Price Bailey, especially in the last twelve years under the leadership of Peter Gillman, has greatly increased the services it can offer. Most recently, it is now authorised to give legal advice.

As it happens, I, the author, have been a client of Price Bailey for 30 years. They have looked after the financial affairs of me personally, as well as my role as an author and as Chairman of my publishing company, Icon Books. I have always enjoyed working with them and have become friends with a number of the partners.

I hope you enjoy reading the book as much as I have enjoyed researching and writing it.

Peter Pugh, June 2013

Author's acknowledgements

Writing, printing and publishing the history of an organisation requires a team effort and the two teams mostly involved, Price Bailey and Icon Books, have made a massive contribution. I interviewed over 50 people, mostly present or former employees of Price Bailey and all, without exception, were very helpful, especially the former Chairman, Richard Price, the former Managing Director now Executive Chairman, Peter Gillman, and the new Managing Director, Martin Clapson.

At Icon Books, the Editorial Director, Duncan Heath, has overseen the project and Marie Doherty and Nick Halliday organised the typesetting and the photographs.

I would like to thank all of them and all the interviewees without whose contributions we would not have had a book.

Peter Pugh, 14 June 2013

Monetary values

Money and its value is always a problem when writing about a period that stretches over a number of years, particularly when parts of that period have included some years of very high inflation. Furthermore, establishing a yardstick for measuring the change in the value of money is not easy either. Do we take the external value of the £ or what it will buy in the average (whatever that may be) weekly shopping basket? Do we relate it to the average manual wage? As we know, while prices in general might rise, and have done so in this country every year since the Second World War, the prices of certain products might fall. However, we are writing about a business, and money and its value crop up on almost every page. We therefore have to make some judgements. We can only generalise, and I think the best yardstick is probably the average working wage.

Taking this as the yardstick, here is a measure of the £ sterling relative to the £ in 2012.

Apart from wartime, prices were stable for 250 years, but prices began to rise in the run-up to the First World War.

1665–1900 multiply by 120	1975–1977 multiply by 15
1900–1914 multiply by 110	1978–1980 multiply by 9
1918–1939 multiply by 60	1980–1987 multiply by 6
1945–1950 multiply by 35	1987–1991 multiply by 3
1950–1960 multiply by 30	1991–1997 multiply by 2
1960–1970 multiply by 25	1997–2013 multiply by 1.5
1970–1974 multiply by 20	

Since 1997, the rate of inflation, by the standards of most of the twentieth century, has been very low, averaging, until very recently, less than the government's originally stated aim of 2.5 per cent (since reduced to 2 per cent). Some things such as telephone charges and many items made in the Far East, notably China, are going down in price while others, such as houses, moved up very sharply from 1997 to 2008 before falling back in the financial crisis. In 2011, on the back of sharply rising commodity and food prices, inflation accelerated again to reach 5 per cent per annum. However, as commodity prices fell back and much of the world suffered very low growth the rate of inflation began to subside again in 2012.

1 | A tough time to start

THE HUNGRY THIRTIES
'I HAVE TO TELL YOU NOW ...'
NO COMPUTERS, NO MOBILES
HAYTERS

THE HUNGRY THIRTIES

The Price Bailey firm of accountants was effectively founded on 2 April 1938 when Leslie Benten opened L.H. Benten & Co. at 6 High Street, Bishop's Stortford. He moved to 1–3 Market Square on 21 March 1939. Benten was joined by Stanley Price in 1943. Price had been born in Bradford in 1917 but the family moved to Bournemouth when he was eight. Stanley's father, Clarence, had married Stanley's mother, Lily. Tragically, Clarence Price was killed in the Battle of Passchendaele in 1917, and Stanley was brought up by his mother who did not marry again. She had been a milliner with her two sisters, Mary and Alice, when they were still in Bradford and opened a milliner's shop when they moved to Bournemouth. Stanley began work articled to an incorporated accountant. Stanley Price became an Articled Clerk of The Society of Incorporated Accountants and Auditors paying £250 [£15,000 in today's money] and signing an agreement on 24 May 1934. There he met his future wife, Barbara, who worked in the practice as a secretary. They moved to Wisbech in north Cambridgeshire where there seemed to be a partnership in prospect for Stanley. However, he did not remain there long and moved to Bishop's Stortford and joined Leslie Benten.

There were a number of farmers in the Bishop's Stortford countryside among the first clients of Benten and Price. One of them was Shrubbs Farm owned by the Liddell family who remained with the practice for over 50 years.

It is easy, and perhaps a relief, to forget the tough economic conditions of 1930s Britain and how hard life was for the majority of people. At the beginning of the decade there had been a world depression of unexpected proportions. This had led to massive unemployment and Britain did not escape. Nor was the suffering confined to the industrial areas of the Midlands, the North of England, South Wales and the industrial areas of Scotland. For example in South-East

2nd. April, 1938.

Dear Sir,

I wish to announce I have severed my connection with Messrs. Trevor Davies & Co. and am continuing in practice at 6 High Street, Bishops Stortford under the style of L. H. Benten & Co.

Yours faithfully,

Letter from Leslie Benten to clients on 2 April 1938.

London, Annie Weaving, the 37 year old wife of an unemployed husband, and mother of seven children, collapsed and died while bathing her six-month old twins. She had been struggling to feed her children and her husband and pay the rent on the 48 shillings (£2.40 or about £100 in today's money) her husband received in benefits. At the inquest the coroner said that, by not eating herself, she had 'sacrificed her life' for the sake of her children.

Statisticians of the time divided the 12 million families in Britain into four social grades, classified according to the chief earner or income receiver in each family.

L. H. BENTEN & CO.

CERTIFIED ACCOUNTANTS.

LESLIE H. BENTEN, A.L.A.A.

TELEPHONE 756.

6, HIGH STREET,

BISHOPS STORTFORD,

HERTS.

21st March, 1939.

Dear Sir,

CHANGE OF ADDRESS

Will you please note our address as from the 23rd March 1939 will be:-

National Provincial Bank Chambers,

1-3, Market Square,

Bishops Stortford,

Herts.

Our telephone number remains unchanged.

Yours faithfully,

L. H. BENTEN & CO.

Letter from Leslie Benten to clients notifying them of his move, 21 March 1939.

	Income of chief earner per week	Number of families	Per cent of families
Class A	Over £10 (£550 in today's money)	635,000	5.2
Class B	£4–£10 (£220–£550)	2,580,000	21.3
Class C	£2 10s–£4 (£137.50–£220)	4,581,000	37.8
Class D	Under £2 10s (£137.50)	4,318,000	35.7

The rich and landed of *Downton Abbey* and *Upstairs, Downstairs* were few and far between!

Life for the middle-class families in Bishop's Stortford was not as bad as this, of course, but nevertheless, businesses were struggling and every effort had to be made to keep down costs. The upper and middle classes were a very small percentage of the population.

Back at L.H. Benten & Co., the fees and balance sheet at the end of the first year of trading were:

	£
Fees	1,130
Postage	15
Telephone	22
Printing and stationery	42
Salaries	289
Rent	54
Profit	708
Balance Sheet	
Motor vehicles	36
Office furniture	60

We need to multiply the numbers by 60 to arrive at today's value. It would therefore look something like this:

	£
Fees	67,800
Postage	900
Telephone	1,320
Printing and stationery	2,520
Salaries	17,340
Rent	3,240
Profit	42,480
Balance Sheet	
Motor vehicles	2,160
Office furniture	3,600

'I HAVE TO TELL YOU NOW ...'

The arguments have raged back and forth for more than 60 years over Britain's preparedness, or lack of it, for war in 1939. In hindsight it is easy to see that a further war with Germany was inevitable, and indeed, the leader of the French army in the First World War, Marshal Foch, described the Treaty of Versailles as merely a twenty-year armistice, a remarkably accurate prediction. However, the spirit of the 1920s and early 1930s was one of peace and goodwill. There had to be a better way to settle men's differences than the appalling slaughter that had taken place between 1914 and 1918. It was not only national revulsion at this carnage that led the British governments of the 1920s and 1930s to reject the isolated calls for rearmament. There was also a widespread feeling, nurtured by such publications as Maynard Keynes's *The Economic Consequences of the Peace*, that Germany had been treated too harshly. And when Hitler began to rant about the injustice of it all, some were inclined to wonder why the Germans scattered around central and eastern Europe should not live under one government. For example, when the German army marched into the demilitarised Rhineland in 1936, Lord Lothian said: 'Hitler is doing no more than taking over his own back garden.'

Foreign Office Intelligence had changed its mind about Germany's preparedness for war. Original calculations suggested a date some time in 1942, but in 1936 fresh information indicated that the Germans might be ready as early as January 1939. This was one of the reasons for the rapid signing of contracts for Hurricanes and Spitfires before either had been fully tested

As we now know, Germany did not invade Poland in January 1939 but at the end of August that year, and the anticipated war was declared on 3 September. By that date, 308 of the 310 Spitfires had been built and tested. What we do not know, and never will, is whether Prime Minister Neville Chamberlain was being Machiavellian when he negotiated with Hitler at Munich in September 1938, knowing full well that Britain was not prepared for war. Historians have disagreed ever since about Chamberlain's motives. For example, A.J.P. Taylor, Britain's populist historian of the 1960s and 1970s, wrote in the *Oxford History of England*, published in 1965:

> The clearest lesson to be drawn from the crisis over Czechoslovakia was that Great Britain should be more heavily armed, whether for negotiation or for war. Chamberlain, a persistent advocate of rearmament, emphasized this lesson strongly and gave Hitler some excuse for complaining that Chamberlain was as insincere in appeasement as Hitler himself was accused of being.

On the other hand, Peter Clarke, Professor of Modern British History at Cambridge, argues in *Hope and Glory, Britain 1900–1990*, that:

> The cynical idea that he was buying time at Munich, put around by some later apologists, had no part in Chamberlain's thinking.

Whatever the truth of his intentions, Chamberlain effectively gave Czechoslovakia to the Germans. Jan Masaryk, the Czech minister for London, said to Lord Halifax, the British Foreign Secretary: 'If you have sacrificed my nation to preserve the peace of the world I will be the first to applaud you. But if not, God help your soul.'

Chamberlain bought another year for Britain, and for Britain's factories to turn out weapons of war. It is generally accepted that the Battle of Britain came within a whisker of being lost, and that this would have left the way open for a German invasion. Certainly, 'Stuffy' Dowding, commander of RAF Fighter Command, had no doubts about the wisdom of Chamberlain's deal with Hitler, saying: 'It was a very good thing that he did act in that way.'

Whether Chamberlain had been a very skilful diplomat or not, on 3 September 1939 he was forced to announce to the British people in sombre tones, these memorable words:

> This morning the British ambassador in Berlin handed the German Government a final Note stating that, unless we heard from them by 11 o'clock that they were prepared to withdraw their troops from Poland, a state of war would exist between us …
>
> … I have to tell you now that no such undertaking has been received and that consequently this country is at war with Germany.

Clearly, maintaining a new accountancy firm through what became a world war and which lasted for nearly six long years was not going to be easy but somehow, Leslie Benten and Stanley Price, who, as we saw, joined him in May 1943, did so. At least they had the compensation that wars are always inflationary and that they were able to put their fees up.

NO COMPUTERS, NO MOBILES

Eventually peace came. What was Britain like when the War finally ended – in Europe in May 1945 and in the Far East in August 1945?

```
LARKING, LARKING & WHITING.
      CHARTERED ACCOUNTANTS.
    ─────────────────

ROLAND C. LARKING, F.C.A., F.S.A.A.
C. GORDON LARKING, F.C.A., A.S.A.A.
WALTER F. WHITING, F.C.A., F.S.A.A.
FRANCIS G.A. COOPER, A.C.A.
ALAN B. SANDAL, A.C.A.


          5/5.
          ─────


          STANLEY PRICE ESQ., A.S.A.A.,
          70, Badgeney Road,
          M A R C H.


Dear Mr. Price,

          I really do not think a reference is
necessary in these days, especially as in your
letter of resignation you say you have been offered
and accepted an appointment.

          As you ask for one, however, I am able to
state that you have been in the employment of this
Firm from the 14th. October 1940, and have given notice
to terminate your employment on the 31st. of this month.

          There is no adverse criticism that I could
make. Your conduct and work have been quite satisfactory.
I am sorry that you are going. You have given no
indication of any dissatisfaction. If you had have done
so I should have done all that I could to remove it.


                    Yours sincerely,
```

```
                          Bridge Buildings,
                              Wisbech.

TELEPHONE NOS ............. 653 ⎱ 2 LINES
                            654 ⎰
AND AT
  BURY ST. EDMUND'S    TEL. NO. 213.
  MARCH            "    " 3107.
  MILDENHALL       "    " 3181.
  PETERBOROUGH     "    " 3507. & RAMSEY.
AND LARKING & LARKING
  CANTERBURY       "    "  377
  LONDON · HOLBORN "    " 2838.
  MAIDSTONE        "    " 4033.
  NORWICH          "    " 3005 ⎱ 2 LINES
                                3006 ⎰
  SITTINGBOURNE    "    "   65.


          WEDNESDAY.
  5th.    May, 1943.
```

Reference for Stanley Price from Larking, Larking and Whiting, 1943.

I cannot improve on what the masterly David Kynaston wrote in his *Austerity Britain 1945–51*:

Britain in 1945. No supermarkets, no motorways, no teabags, no sliced bread, no frozen food, no flavoured crisps, no lager, no microwaves, no dishwashers, no Formica, no vinyl, no CDs, no computers, no mobiles, no duvets, no Pill, no trainers, no hoodies, no Starbucks. Four Indian restaurants. Shops on every corner, pubs on every corner, cinemas in every high street, red telephone boxes, Lyons

Corner Houses, trams, trolleybuses, steam trains. Woodbines, Craven 'A', Senior Service, smoke, smog, Vapex inhalant. No launderettes, no automatic washing machines, wash day every Monday, clothes boiled in a tub, scrubbed on the draining board, rinsed in the sink, put through the mangle, hung out to dry. Central heating rare, coke boilers, water geysers, the coal fire, the hearth, the home, chilblains common. Abortion illegal, homosexual relationships illegal, suicide illegal, capital punishment legal. White faces everywhere. Back-to backs, narrow cobble streets, Victorian terraces, no high-rises. Arterial roads, suburban semis, the march of the pylon. Austin Sevens, Ford Eights, no seat belts, Triumph motorcycles with sidecars. A Bakelite wireless in the home, Housewives' Choice or Workers' Playtime or ITMA on the air, televisions almost unknown, no programmes to watch, the family eating together. Milk of Magnesia, Vick Vapour Rub, Friar's Balsam, Fynnon Salts, Eno's, Germolene. Suits and hats, dresses and hats, cloth caps and mufflers, no leisurewear, no 'teenagers'. Heavy coins, heavy shoes, heavy suitcases, heavy tweed coats, heavy leather footballs, no unbearable lightness of being. Meat rationed, butter rationed, lard rationed, margarine rationed, sugar rationed, tea rationed, cheese rationed, jam rationed, eggs rationed, sweets rationed, soap rationed, clothes rationed. Make do and mend.

In terms of government, to many people's surprise, the voters rejected the Conservatives and their leader, Winston Churchill and gave a landslide victory to the Labour Party. Whereas the attitude in 1918 had been one of trying to return to the golden pre-war era, in 1945 few wanted to return to the 1930s.

Stanley Price became a partner at L.H. Benten on Christmas Eve 1946 and, shortly afterwards, the firm opened a second office at Gothic House in Old Harlow. On 1 April 1950 Reginald Bailey was appointed a partner and the firm became known as Benten, Price and Bailey. The Bishop's Stortford office moved to the Guild House. In 1956 a Cambridge office was opened in Kinneard Way and Leslie Benten left the practice on 30 September 1956.

Stanley Price worked closely with Jim Tee of Tees, the solicitors in Bishop's Stortford (now in Cambridge, Chelmsford, Great Dunmow, Northampton and Saffron Walden as well) and one of the current partners, David Redfern, reckons that Tees were considered THE solicitors in Bishop's Stortford, while Price Bailey were considered THE accountants. Jim Tee and Stanley Price were admired as 'men of affairs' giving wise advice.

All three partners must have been close in the 1950s because Stanley's son, Richard, can remember going to both the Benten and Bailey houses on social occasions. In Richard's view, Reg Bailey was the meticulous partner while his father, Stanley Price, was more adventurous.

BANK CHAMBERS,
1-3, MARKET SQUARE,
BISHOP'S STORTFORD
HERTS.

24th December, 1946.

Dear Sir (Madam),

I have much pleasure in informing you that as from the 1st January, 1947, I am taking into partnership Mr. Stanley Price, Incorporated Accountant, who has been with me for several years as Managing Clerk, and is well known to most of my Clients.

The firm will continue to practice under the style of "L. H. Benten & Co." at the above address and at Market Row, Saffron Walden, Essex, and as from the 1st January, 1947 we shall also have offices at Gothic House, High Street, Harlow, Essex, and 4, Guildhall Place, Cambridge.

Yours faithfully,

Letter from Leslie Benten to clients telling them he has made Stanley Price a partner as of 1 January 1947. It also shows that L.H. Benten & Co. had an office in Saffron Walden and their intention to open in Harlow and Cambridge on 1 January 1947.

Richard began to do some work in the Benten, Price & Bailey office in the school holidays in 1956 when he was 11 years old. Everything was manual in those days and he remembered that even in the early 1960s when he commenced his articles in the City, the only aids they had were an abacus and slide-rule.

Richard can remember that they would often go to clients at the weekend to have lunch and enjoy the day with them. One of the firm's clients was the farming family, the Everetts. There was no electricity on the farm and the toilet facilities were outside. He could also remember playing tennis with one of the client's family and that presents such as a chicken were sometimes given to his father.

Richard would say later, 'Leslie Benten did not like the effort being put into

Harlow and Cambridge and went off to Saffron Walden to set up a new L.H. Benten & Co.'

The firm was renamed Price Bailey and Partners. Don Holledge and Stan Trow were appointed partners. Holledge did not stay long. These were the terms of the Dissolution agreement signed by Holledge, Reg Bailey, Stanley Price and Stan Trow on 23 November 1960:

2. The Purchasers agree to purchase the share and interest of Outgoing Partner in the goodwill of the said business from the Thirtieth day of September One thousand nine hundred and sixty at the price of Six thousand eight hundred and fifty six pounds together with such sum as may stand to the credit of the Outgoing Partner on capital account on the said Thirtieth day of September One thousand nine hundred and sixty after debiting him with any liabilities for taxation.

3. The said purchase money shall be satisfied in manner following namely – Partly by the Purchasers securing the release of the Outgoing Partner from the sum of One thousand five hundred pounds owing by the Outgoing Partner to the Century Insurance Company Limited together with the release by the Century Insurance Company of the policy of One thousand five hundred pounds on the life of the Outgoing Partner – Partly by the Purchasers securing the release of the Outgoing Partner from the sum of Two thousand six hundred pounds owing by the Outgoing Partner to Leslie Herbert Benten – Partly by the Covenant of the Purchasers to pay the Outgoing Partner the balance of the said purchase money namely the sum of Two thousand seven hundred and fifty six pounds and the amount standing to his credit on capital account as aforesaid by eighty equal quarterly instalments commencing on the First day of January One thousand nine hundred and sixty one with interest on the balance for the time being unpaid at the rate of one per cent above Bank Rate such covenant to be contained in a Deed of Covenant to be executed by the Purchasers.[The sums of money mentioned need to be multiplied by 30 to see what they were in today's terms]

Following Holledge's departure a new agreement was drawn up with Stan Trow which also included Tom Parkin,

W H E R E A S :

1. Mr Price, Mr Bailey, Donald Arthur Holledge and Mr Trow have heretofore carried on the profession of Accountants at Bishop's Stortford in the County of Hertford (hereinafter called 'the Stortford Practice')————————————

2.   Mr Price has heretofore carried on the profession of an Accountant at Harlow in the County of Essex (hereinafter called 'the Harlow Practice')————

3.   Mr Bailey has heretofore carried on the profession of an Accountant in the Town and County of Cambridge (hereinafter called 'the Cambridge Practice')——

4.   The parties have hereto agreed to amalgamate the Stortford, Harlow and Cambridge Practices as from the First day of October One thousand nine hundred and sixty————

5.   The Stortford Practice is subject to a Mortgage in favour of The Century Insurance Company Limited to secure the sum of Six thousand four hundred and seventy five pounds and the Harlow Practice is subject to a Mortgage in favour of The Century Insurance Company Limited to secure the sum of One thousand pounds————

6.   It is proposed to secure the said sums of Six thousand four hundred and seventy five pounds and One thousand pounds together with the further advance of Six thousand five hundred and twenty five pounds hereinafter mentioned on the new firm————

NOW IT IS HEREBY AGREED as follows:

1.   As a result of the amalgamation of the Stortford Practice, the Harlow Practice and the Cambridge Practice as from the First day of October One thousand nine hundred and sixty Mr Bailey owes Mr Price the sum of Four thousand nine hundred and thirty seven pounds ten shillings and Mr Trow owes Mr Price the sum of Six thousand six hundred and eighty seven pounds ten shillings————

2.   The parties hereto will enter into Articles of Partnership in the form of the draft already initialled by them————

3.   Tom Parkin (hereinafter called 'Mr Parkin') at present employed by the Harlow Practice will be admitted to the new firm as soon as he has qualified as a Chartered Accountant Mr Price agreeing to sell him a ten per cent interest in the profits of the new firm for Two thousand and fifty pounds Mr Trow agreeing to sell him a seven and a half per cent interest in the profits of the new firm for Five thousand two hundred and eighty seven pounds ten shillings————

4.   A further advance of Six thousand five hundred and twenty five pounds shall be raised from The Century Insurance Company Limited on the security of the new firm making a total advance of Fourteen thousand pounds and the said sum of Six thousand five hundred and twenty five pounds shall be applied as to Four thousand nine hundred and thirty seven pounds ten shillings in satisfaction of the amount due from Mr Bailey to Mr Price and as to One thousand five hundred and eighty seven pounds ten shillings in part satisfaction of the amount due from Mr Trow to Mr Price leaving a balance of Five thousand one hundred pounds due from Mr Trow to Mr Price————————————————————

5.   On the sale by Mr Trow to Mr Parkin of a seven and a half per cent share in the profits of the new firm the purchase money of Five thousand two hundred and eighty seven pounds ten shillings be applied in satisfaction of any sum then due from Mr Trow to Mr Price————————————————————

6.   Until the said sum of Five thousand one hundred pounds have been satisfied Mr Trow agrees to pay Mr Price or to his personal representatives the said sum of Five thousand one hundred pounds by eighty equal quarterly instalments on the First day of January the First day of April the First day of July and the First day of October in each year the first of such quarterly payments to be made on the First day of January One thousand nine hundred and sixty one together with interest on the balance for the time being remaining unpaid at the rate of one per cent above Bank Rate for the time being in force until the whole of the said sums and interest as aforesaid shall be fully paid————————————

HAYTERS

While Stanley Price was helping to build up Price Bailey, he also became an adviser and non-executive financial director of Hayters which became one of Bishop's Stortford's leading manufacturing companies.

Hayters had been founded by Douglas Hayter in 1946. This is how he told the story of its beginnings:

In the hot summer of 1946 I needed to clear my builder's yard in Spellbrook on the Hertfordshire-Essex border, which was overgrown with grass. I had no mower of my own so I borrowed a friend's cutter bar machine. It was hopeless and I spent more time repairing it than cutting grass. I decided to build a mower myself.

This first rotary mower was the foundation of Hayters which became THE name in world-class rotary mowers. To research the first machine, Douglas Hayter went to the Science Museum in London where he found records of a rotary machine powered by a horse. He combined a second-hand, two-stroke engine with various bits and pieces from under his workshop bench. He used a dustbin lid to guard the blade! Within 24 hours the Hayter rotary mower was ready for testing. It was so effective that a neighbour asked Hayter to make one for him and that is how Hayters started.

Kim Macfie with the famous Hayter rotary mower. Both Stanley and Richard Price
served as Finance Director and helped Hayters achieve great success.

Hayters' Orchard Mower, exhibited at the Royal Smithfield Show at Earl's Court in 1950.

By the mid-1960s Hayters was turning over £1 million (over £25 million in today's money) and by the early 1980s was a public company with sales of £6 million (about £30 million in today's money) and profits of £750,000 (nearly £4 million). The prospectus for a placement of shares said of Stanley Price's role:

> Mr S Price, aged 64, is a non-executive Finance Director. He is the senior partner in a local firm of Chartered Accountants, and he has advised the company since incorporation. He fulfils the usual duties of a non-executive director and, in particular, advises on finance and accounting matters.

When Stanley Price retired from Price Bailey in 1982, he also retired as non-executive Finance Director of Hayters and Douglas Hayter said of his long service:

Stanley Price has been connected with Hayters since the company's formation in November 1946. He was appointed a non-executive director in 1953 and has played an invaluable role in directing the financial affairs of the company over the years.

The press release announcing Stanley Price's retirement went on to say that he would be succeeded by his son Richard Price:

A local man, Mr Price, aged 38, was educated at Bishop's Stortford College and trained with a city firm of chartered accountants, qualifying in 1969.

He then joined the same firm of Price Bailey and Partners, becoming a partner in 1974. Currently, he is on the Education Committee of the South Essex Society of Chartered Accountants and is County Chairman of Hertfordshire Round Tables. He is married with two children and lives in Dane Park, Bishop's Stortford.

As well as acting as Finance Director of Hayters Mowers, Richard Price was also the Finance Director of Aid Pallets Ltd in Hoddesden. He would say later:

Working with these two companies made me realise how insensitive auditors could be when dealing with their clients and I made sure that the Price Bailey teams took care to avoid such insensitivity.

When Hayters was taken over by F.H. Tomkins plc in 1985, the Chief Executive, Greg Hutchings, wrote this to Richard Price:

Dear Richard,

I would like to thank you personally for all you have done for Hayters, before during and after our acquisition, in particular, I am very grateful for the part you played at the time of the acquisition when I believe that in a totally professional way you acted very efficiently and effectively on behalf of Doug Hayter. Ian and I respect you very much for this.

I do hope that we will continue to maintain a close contact with you even though you have ceased to be a non-executive Director of Hayters.

I know that Jim Sanger values your advice and I am sure that Ivan and the new Finance Director will continue to want your help. I have asked Jim to agree a method of working together with you as soon as possible after the Finance Director has arrived.

Thank you Richard, for all your help in the past ... and hopefully in the future.

Douglas Hayter died in October 2000 and Richard Price wrote this to his wife, Susan:

Dear Susan

Douglas and my family go back a long way, with my father helping Douglas from the earliest days of Hayters. They spent a lot of time together and had a high regard for one another. The business grew so well, with its innovative products designed and enthusiastically produced by Douglas. His selling of his idea was outstanding and it led to the name and products of Hayters being known world-wide. I remember the interest we, as a family, had in spotting the agency sign or Hayter machines when we were abroad. I remember in particular not only seeing a lot of Douglas at Spellbrook, but also at Loddon and Wroxham with other sides of the business. He was always enthusiastic about the products, if not always about some of the personnel who tried to keep up with him and his ideas. My strongest recollections are when I was Finance Director and we planned the disposal of the company and travelled the country together trying to find the right buyer. It was a busy and interesting time, but I often felt Douglas found it very difficult to give up his company. I cannot say I was pleased at his or anyone else's treatment by Tomkins after the agreement was concluded, but it was a great deal which continued to keep the Hayter products in a world-wide context, which was and is a great tribute to their inventor and mentor. Douglas was always fair, although sometimes difficult, but I respected him enormously – he was a great man.

2 | Up and down the A11

A GOOD LOCATION
'FIRST PRIZE IN THE LOTTERY OF LIFE'
EXPANSION ALONG THE A11
THE CAMBRIDGE PHENOMENON
MOVING TOWARDS LONDON

A GOOD LOCATION

As the partners of Price Bailey discovered, Bishop's Stortford, in East Hertfordshire, was very well located for expansion in East Anglia and indeed, eventually into London and therefore, overseas.

On the A11 main road, and now just west of the M11 motorway, it is very close to London Stansted Airport. It is just 29 miles north east of Charing Cross, long considered the central point of London. The main railway line from Cambridge to Liverpool Street Station runs through Bishop's Stortford. In the *Channel 4* 'Best and worst places to live in the UK' East Hertfordshire was voted seventh best. (See Chapter 7 for the benefits Price Bailey reaped from the expansion of Stansted Airport from the 1980s onwards.)

Originally called Esterteford, this was gradually shortened to Stortford and, in 1060, William, Bishop of London, bought the Stortford manor and estate for eight pounds. The town has been known as Bishop's Stortford ever since. The local river was named Stort after the town and it was made navigable in 1769. At about the same time the town became a stagecoach stop on the mail coach road between Cambridge and London. By 1801 Bishop's Stortford had become a market town with a corn exchange. The main industry was malting. In 1842 the railway arrived.

The twentieth century brought strong population growth. In 1901 the town's population was still only 7,000. By 1951 it was 13,000 and by the 2001 census it was 35,000. Steady growth has continued since then.

'FIRST PRIZE IN THE LOTTERY OF LIFE'

Bishop's Stortford's most famous citizen was Cecil Rhodes who was born, the fifth son of the Reverend Francis Rhodes, in 1853. Francis Rhodes was a Church of England vicar who always boasted of never having delivered a sermon of longer than 10 minutes. Cecil became a sickly, asthmatic adolescent and was taken out of grammar school and sent to Natal in South Africa where, it was hoped, the hot climate would improve his health. He worked on the cotton farm managed by his older brother, Herbert. He arrived in Natal on 1 September 1870 and, after a year, moved to the diamond fields of Kimberley which were just opening up.

For the next 17 years, financed by N.M. Rothschild & Sons, Rhodes bought up all the smaller diamond mining operations in the Kimberley area. In 1889 his monopoly of the world's diamond supply was achieved through a partnership with the London based Diamond Syndicate. Two of his early colleagues were John Merriman and Charles Rudd who later became his partner in the De Beers Mining Company and Niger Oil Company.

Rhodes went from strength to strength and founded De Beers which at one time marketed 90 per cent of the world's rough diamonds. It still markets 40 per cent. A strong believer in the British Empire, he founded the state of Rhodesia which was named after him, as was South Africa's Rhodes University. He set up

Cecil Rhodes's birthplace in Bishop's Stortford.

the Rhodes Scholarships allowing overseas students to study at Oxford University which are still funded by his estate. There have been thousands of beneficiaries including Bill Clinton, former President of the USA.

THE RHODES COLOSSUS

Cecil Rhodes bestrides Africa. His ambition was that the British should colonise the whole of the African continent.

Rhodes was the ultimate British imperialist. His British South Africa Company annexed Mashonoland and Matabeleland to form Rhodesia. He is supposed to have said: 'To be born an Englishman is to win first prize in the lottery of life.'

He definitely did say: 'All of those stars … these vast worlds that remain out of reach. If I could, I would annex other planets.'

Richard Price's earliest memories of Price Bailey were at the Market Square offices in the early 1950s. Apparently there was a large room which had wooden slatted shelves all around the room. On these shelves, paper parcels and some boxes held clients' records. The brown paper parcels were tied with string and secured with sealing wax. There were no computers but rather manual typewriters. Any alterations had to be made using ink rubbers. The accounts were typed on sheets of A3 paper. There were two secretaries with manual typewriters working there. One of these ladies, Mrs Valerie Bayford, came and baby sat Richard and his brother when their parents went out.

Richard remembers going to Saffron Walden to Leslie Benten's home for lunches and playing in the garden. He also remembers going to Reg Bailey's home in Bishop's Stortford and later in Cambridge and playing with Susan

The Black Bull Inn (Price Bailey's present office is located just beyond where this pub was) in Bishop's Stortford in the 1890s.

Bailey and even holding a small baby – Lawrence Bailey! He also went to the home of Tom Parkin, one of the office managers.

When he went to Waterside School at the age of five, he would walk along the Causeway, Bridge Street and Water Lane to the new office at The Guild House and wait for his father to drive him home. This was a much larger office with many rooms and a staircase. There were outside lavatories at the rear. Later an extension was added to provide four more offices on two floors as well as internal lavatories.

Richard's first working experience was from the age of 11 for a few years when he would work for a couple of weeks each summer holidays for some pocket money. He learnt to add cash books in pounds, shillings and pence. He became quite good at this and he always had the skill to add up more quickly in his head than on an adding machine, which came into use many years later.

Richard also remembers two of the early partners, Stan Trow, a thin, dapper man, and Don Holledge, a larger man and very kind. Lesley Benten, Stanley Price and Tom Parkin always seemed to be smoking pipes.

A new office was opened in Cambridge, at 2 Glisson Road, in 1962. Vernon Clarke, who had been the firm's first articled clerk, was appointed a partner on

The Congregational Chapel in Bishop's Stortford at the end of the nineteenth century
(Price Bailey occupied the building in the background).

(this page) North Street, Bishop's Stortford in the 1930s.

(opposite page, top) North Street, Bishop's Stortford in the early 1950s.

(opposite page, bottom) Richard Price can remember visiting the Price Bailey offices in the Guild House, Bishop's Stortford in the 1950s.

NORTH STREET, BISHOP'S STORTFORD. (7) 215238. J.V.

NORTH STREET, BISHOPS STORTFORD

Four young employees outside Price Bailey's office in the Guild House, Bishop's Stortford in 1960. From left to right: Tony Saban (eventually a partner), Derek Francis, David Midgeley and Robert Bridgeman.

1 April 1964. Richard can remember that Vernon Clarke would cycle from Sawbridgeworth to the Bishop's Stortford office and also to the Harlow office during the week and on alternate Saturday mornings. Furthermore, the telephone switchboard was manned in all the offices on Saturday mornings. He can also remember that lunch was an important event and that the partners went out to lunch every day.

Clarke was followed as a partner on 1 October 1966 by Norman Hall, a tax specialist from Peat Marwick, and on 1 October 1967 by Graham Hardy when Stan Trow retired.

An office was opened in Great Dunmow in 1969 and the following year Michael Horwood and Graham Savage were appointed partners. A further big expansion took place on 1 June 1974 when Richard Price, Roger Evans and Nigel Bailey (Reg's nephew) were appointed partners, while Tony Saban, Mike Nicholls and Bill Roberts became profit sharing managers. The following year Andrew Hulme was appointed a partner and Peter Bass a profit sharing manager. In 1976 an office was opened in Chingford in Essex and, in 1978, an office was opened in Chesterton, on the outskirts of Cambridge.

Mike Nicholls, who had joined the firm at the Bishop's Stortford office in 1967 after qualifying as a certified accountant while working for Huntingdon County Council, remembered that the majority of clients were small businesses and included farmers, builders, doctors and dentists. For example, a small builder, Helmet and Dyer, had been a client since 1939.

Also in 1962 Price Bailey employed Graham Hardy who would serve until his retirement as Chairman in 1996 having become the first Managing Partner in 1991. This was how he remembered the firm in the 1960s:

My first contact with the firm was at an interview for a senior position at Bishop's Stortford in October 1962. I met Stanley Price and Stanley Trow, the then partners, at the Guild House on the first floor before the building was extended. I felt the interview had gone well as Stanley Price had known the boss of the firm I trained with, Denis Rawlinson & Co. in Peterborough, as at one time, although they may not have met, they had both worked for Larking, Larking and Whiting.

As I was due to take my final exams in November and as my wife, Dianne, and I were expecting out first child in January 1963 I didn't want to move until our daughter had safely arrived. In a few days I received a letter saying that they couldn't really wait until then to fill the vacancy at Bishop's Stortford but expected to have a position which they could offer me at Harlow and invited us to visit them there. The employee I was to replace didn't yet know he was to leave!

We went shortly afterwards and I again met Stanley Price and Tom Parkin, the manager of the Harlow office. They showed us round the town which was one of the new towns being built around London in the 1950s and 1960s. One of the attractions of the town for us was the opportunity to be able to rent a house, which would have been built by the Harlow Development Corporation.

I was offered and accepted a senior position at the Harlow office and we moved into a new house at the beginning of March 1963. I was given a small portfolio of clients to deal with and soon formed the opinion that in a number of practical ways my new firm was some way ahead of my old firm.

Stanley Price had been a partner in Benten, Price and Bailey at Bishops Stortford for some time and had had the foresight to open an office in Old Harlow and later in The Stow in Harlow as the new town was being built, calling it Price and Bailey. In 1960 the firm had moved into new offices at Aylmer House, The High, which was the new town centre. I soon realised that he believed in developing the practice through personal contacts and that he knew many of the senior officers of the Development Corporation and of other professional firms in the town. One of the positions that he held on a voluntary basis was Treasurer of the Harlow and District Sports Trust which was established in 1959 to build and operate a sportcentre.

Stanley Price's work for the Sports Trust was highly appreciated as these comments in a letter from a committee member in July 1968 show clearly:

Though you have often pretended not to be keeping up I have always known how splendidly you have in fact been backing up all the time, and that your expert knowledge and advice have been behind the younger chaps you have pushed forward. Apart from everything else this has been a tremendous contribution, and it is entirely due to you that we are able to appoint someone as competent as Graham Hardy to carry on. He seems dedicated and conscious that all our problems are not easy ones.

Graham Hardy said of his association with the Trust:

In 1965 he asked me to be Assistant Treasurer to the Sports Trust which I was happy to do as I had always been very keen on sport. Not that I was any good, but over the years I was able to play squash there and also much later a few over 50s cricket matches. As the years progressed I took over the position of Treasurer and later I became Chairman for a ten year period from 1982.

Initially, Graham worked under Tom Parkin and said of him:

Tom Parkin came from Appleby in Westmoreland and had started his training in accountancy before the war with Armstrong Watson in Carlisle. He had joined the armed forces and so had never taken his final exams. However he was accepted as a partner in all but name and his salary was related to the profits of the firm. He was another major influence in my life and gave me a lot of encouragement, including me in a number of social gatherings where I met many of the leaders of local authority and industry. He was a member of the Rotary Club of Harlow and invited me to join the club in 1971. His early death from cancer in 1974 at the age of 51 devastated me but it left me in charge of the office.

Brought up in Peterborough and educated at King's School, Peterborough, Graham had enjoyed holidays in the West Country and he and his wife wanted to live there (and indeed, do now live there in retirement). He attended interviews with accounting practices in both Bristol and Bridgewater but the attraction of Price Bailey in Bishop's Stortford was the offer of their renting a house owned by the firm. In 1966 he received two approaches from people he had trained with to join them but, as he said:

We had just bought our first house, that would have been difficult and I had turned them down. Stanley and Tom told me they hoped that I would stay with the firm and become a partner, which I did in 1967. At the same time Stanley Trow left the firm to join another firm in the south of England. Reginald Bailey had opened the firm's office in Cambridge under the name R.E. Bailey & Son and at this time all three offices changed the name of the firm to Price Bailey and Partners.

Before I became a partner Norman Hall joined the practice in 1966. He lived in Bishop's Stortford and was previously with a large city firm for some years. He brought some much needed tax expertise to the firm.

He became a partner on 1 October 1967 when Stan Trow retired and remembers that all the partners from Bishop's Stortford, Cambridge and Harlow used to meet at the Bishop's Stortford office every Thursday morning and work out the time spent on each client and decide what invoices to send them. Graham Hardy himself was charging out his time at £6 an hour [£150 an hour in today's money].

EXPANSION ALONG THE A11

Price Bailey's expansion along the A11 was steady from 1947 through the 1950s, 1960s, 1970s and 1980s.

In 1947 a second office was opened in Old Harlow. The town can trace its history back into BC times but it came to national notice when it was one of the towns developed after the Second World War to ease overcrowding in London. The development incorporated the market town of Harlow, now a neighbourhood known as Old Harlow, as well as a number of nearby villages. The town was divided into neighbourhoods, each self-supporting with their own shopping precincts, community facilities and public house. Harlow could boast the first pedestrian precinct and first modern-style residential tower-block in the UK. In 1954, Price Bailey relocated to 120 The Stow, which was the first pedestrian precinct in the country, and, in 1961, to Aylmer House in The High.

The next important move was in Cambridge.

THE CAMBRIDGE PHENOMENON

Employment opportunities in Cambridge in the 1950s and 1960s were restricted to a few distinct sectors. The university dominated the town, not only the academic staff who generally lived within the confines of college or in the smarter west or south side of Cambridge, but many hundreds of porters, cooks, bed-makers, gardeners, cleaners and other college servants who mainly lived in the poorer east and northern parts of the town.

The shops and service trades, as in any provincial market town, provided a living for many, together with the usual professions of solicitors, doctors, dentists, school teachers and estate agents. There were the City and County Councils in the Guildhall and County Hall at the top of Castle Hill. Cambridge-based regional government congregated in the side roads off Brooklands Avenue.

The small amount of industry which existed was highly specialised. W.G. Pye started out as manufacturers of scientific instruments for the Cavendish Laboratories but then expanded into wider electrical goods in the Granta Works in Chesterton. Pye Telecommunications Ltd flourished in the 1950s and 1960s, and employed hundreds of skilled workers, until they were taken over by Phillips in 1976 and undone by Far East competition. Cambridge Consultants had been

In 1962 a new office was opened in Glisson Road, Cambridge.

founded in 1960, 'to put the brains of Cambridge University at the disposal of the problems of British Industry'.

Out on the Harston Road was Fison Agrochemicals plant where they made pesticides and fertilisers, and ruined the setting of the once picturesque Hauxton Mill next door. CIBA had a similar factory out at Duxford. At Barrington there was the cement works. The only industry which offered opportunities for unskilled or casual work was Chivers Jam factory in Histon.

In 1969 the Mott Report recommended the expansion of science-based industries close to Cambridge and in 1970, Trinity College decided to develop their own land off Milton Road as a new science park. This huge site, beside the Northern bypass, and now home to over 100 high-tech firms, has been the biggest factor in the growth of the 'Cambridge Phenomenon' of 'Silicon Fen'. The university's own West Cambridge project alongside the Western bypass off Madingley Road will provide yet more growth. While Chivers Jam factory in Histon and Fisons at Hauxton have closed, thousands of people now work in new cleaner and better-paid research, development and manufacturing companies.

The transition from the austerity and insularity of Cambridge in the 1950s to the prosperity and opportunity of the last decade has been extraordinary. There can be nowhere in Britain where Harold Wilson's 'white heat of technology' has been more completely realised.

Perhaps the biggest change of all in the character and role of Cambridge over the last thirty years has been the growth of commuting to London. The electrification of the King's Cross line, which used to be slower even than the old diesel trains into Liverpool Street Station, coupled with the perceived quality of life, has turned Cambridge and its hinterland into a London dormitory. The attractiveness of Cambridge as 'a nice place to live' caused property prices to rocket to smart-London levels. The demand for new housing appeared insatiable.

Much of this growth, after the completion of New Chesterton and the Arbury/King's Hedges estate, has been in the villages. Those which were allocated village colleges before the war, such as Sawston, Bottisham, Linton, Comberton and Impington/Histon were planned long ago to become mini-towns and have become exactly that. In 1964 a further new 'village' was proposed at Bar Hill, five miles north-west along the Huntingdon Road. In the boom years of the early 1970s and mid-1980s Bar Hill expanded at over 200 new houses per year. In 1977 a Tesco supermarket replaced the village shop, and when it was rebuilt again in 2001 it was for a few weeks the largest superstore in the country. So much for keeping things local! The new giant Waitrose at Trumpington has also added to the confused picture of car-driven shopping in Cambridge.

Cambridge was once regarded as a rural backwater that happened to house a world-class university. However, the town and region have experienced above-average economic growth from the 1960s onwards. Indeed, it has become one of the fastest growing economies in the UK. In 2000 unemployment was half the national average while GDP per head was 25 per cent more. Earnings in the Cambridge area were about 10 per cent higher than the rest of England. This economic growth attracted people into the Cambridge region and the population grew from 260,000 in 1951 to nearly half a million by 2010.

One of the big growth factors has been that of high-tech companies known as *The Cambridge Phenomenon*. The number of high-tech companies in the area grew from 261 with 13,700 employees in 1984 to 600 with 20,000 employees in 1990 to 1,250 with 32,500 employees in 1998. The Phenomenon was largely a creation of the 1970s and 1980s although there had been earlier spin-offs from the Cambridge University laboratories. For example, Cambridge Instruments had been founded as early as 1881 and W.G. Pye left Cavendish Laboratories in 1896 to found his own company, eventually taken over by the Dutch electronics giant Philips.

1967 was a key date when Cambridge University set up a committee to advise on its relationship with science-based industry. The Mott Report, published in 1969, proposed allowing science and research-based industries to grow. This enabled changes to the County Development Plan and the development of the Trinity Science Park and other industrial developments. Two important firms, Cambridge Consultants Ltd and Applied Research of Cambridge had been founded in the 1960s and, with encouragement and help from the banks, in particular Barclays Bank in Bene't Street, many others followed in the 1970s and 1980s.

During the 1980s and 1990s there were some casualties, notably Ionica in 1998 with the loss of 700 jobs, but by 1998 there were 1,250 high-tech firms employing more than 30,000 people in the Cambridge area. Furthermore, for the new millennium there were several new developments such as Granta Park with around 50,000 square metres of office space available on 26 hectares, Cambridge University's West Cambridge site with 41,000 square metres of office space, Babraham's Institute with its 26,000 square metre biopark, Cambourne Business Park with 70,000 square metres, Cambridge Research Park with 56,000 square metres and Addenbrooke's Hospital for companies linked to drug and medical research.

As we have seen, Price Bailey had opened an office in Cambridge when Reginald Bailey moved into Kinnaird Way. Lawrence Bailey would say of this move:

Dad (Reginald Bailey) and Stanley (Price) were quite happy working in Bishop's Stortford. There was terrific chemistry between them. My grandfather had run Eastern Electrical Wiring Company and my parents lived there. My father started to get a number of clients in the city and then built himself a house in Kinnaird Way in 1957, which was where the Cambridge office started, two days a week from his front room.

Reg Bailey went to the County High School in Cambridge and initially worked for the accountancy firm Slater, Dominy and Storm, who were eventually taken over by Spicer and Pegler, now called Deloittes. He qualified in the late 1940s and joined Leslie Benten and Stanley Price in 1950. At the time the firm had offices in Bishop's Stortford, Saffron Walden and Ramsey in north Cambridgeshire where they had taken over a firm called Youndle. The Baileys were living in Bishop's Stortford when their son, Lawrence Bailey, who would eventually join and become a partner in Price Bailey, was born in 1949. The Bailey family moved to Kinnaird Way in Cambridge in 1957 and Price Bailey's first Cambridge client was Peak's Furnishers in Fitzroy Street.

Keith Peak remembered that he had been so impressed by Reg Bailey, who had made a cold call offering his services in 1952, that he went to the company's current accountants, picked up the accountancy books and took them over to Reg.

A Peak's Furnishers van in the 1960s. Keith Peak was very impressed by Reg Bailey when he met him.

The Peak business at the time was primarily a large furniture retail store in an area on Fitzroy Street, Cambridge known as 'The Kite' and in Bradwells Court. Alec Forshaw in his book *Growing up in Cambridge,* wrote this of Peak's:

In Fitzroy Street was Peak's Furnitures where my parents inspected and bought the utility furniture that stocked our house, simple and 'modern' with no frills, much more fashionable today than it ever was then.

In the 1980s recession Peak's hit hard times. They sold their retail outlets and were trading as 'The Storehouse' offering a large range of branded furniture to the trade throughout the country. Margins were small, much was bought from Denmark which devalued and in 1982 Peak's went into voluntary liquidation. Fortunately, they were able to start again offering commercial and archive storage and thanked Tony Saban of Price Bailey and a consultant, Arnold Backwith, who was introduced by Richard Price, for their help and advice.

Price Bailey took advantage of the opportunities as Cambridge grew and

Cintra House, the Price Bailey Cambridge office location in the 1970s.

gradually opened new and larger offices. In 1962 the office moved to 2 Glisson Road as it made its first major acquisition, Dickersons. In 1965 it moved to Bradwells Court and in 1970 to Cintra House in Hills Road. It opened another office at 198 Green End Road in Chesterton in 1978. There was a feeling that Cambridge needed an accountancy office north of the river and, furthermore, the office in Cintra House was becoming crowded. Lawrence Bailey was asked to manage the new office 'under the supervision of the Cambridge partners.' It then moved first to 98 Regent Street and then in 1982 to 93 Regent Street. Finally, it moved to the Quorum on the edge of Marshall's Airport in 2004.

MOVING TOWARDS LONDON

In 1969 Price Bailey opened in Great Dunmow in Essex, a town less than 10 miles from both Bishop's Stortford and Braintree. This town could trace its history back to Roman times when it was a small Roman town on the road which ran south-west to London and north-west to Cambridge. By the time of the Domesday Book, Dunmow had seven manors, some of which still exist. In the Middle Ages the town flourished with market charters granted in 1253 and two fairs held annually until the nineteenth century.

The Second World War brought plenty of action to the town as it was situated on the GHQ Line, a series of defences and concrete pillboxes built to hinder a possible German invasion. Many are still visible along the Chelmer Valley. Easton Lodge became RAF Great Dunmow during the War and also housed squadrons of the US Air Force. Post-war the town has prospered especially when Stansted Airport was developed.

The story of Nigel Bailey, nephew of Reg, has to be included in a history of Price Bailey. Unsavoury though it is, the way it was handled by the other partners illustrates the integrity of the firm.

In the early 1970s Nigel Bailey was the sole partner in the Great Dunmow office. By 1974 the other partners in the firm were expressing concern about the numbers coming out of the Dunmow office. Following a meeting of the partners when Nigel could not attend because he was on holiday, Richard Price was sent to the Dunmow office to ask Nigel for more information and he was to stay there until he was satisfied that he understood what had been going on. As he said later: 'It was quite tricky because we were godparents of each other's children.'

It was discovered that Nigel had been manipulating the figures and stealing money from the firm and from clients. To their great credit, Price Bailey did not try to cover things up but informed both the Institute of Chartered Accountants

Old Bank House in Great Dunmow, home of the Price Bailey Dunmow office from 1975 until 1996.

and the police. Nigel Bailey was prosecuted, found guilty and given a prison sentence, suspended for three years.

The episode did have an effect on the firm. Richard Price said:

> Partners worked nights to recover the situation. Any clients who had lost money were paid back. One or two stopped using the firm and we probably lost a few potential clients.

The next office to open was Chingford in 1976. There have been many suggestions as to how the name arose, many of them associated with the River Ching. In the end the most generally accepted view is that Shingly Ford was the origin and means a ford over a river containing shingles.

This move still stuck to expansion along the A11 but it was now getting close to London. Indeed, it features in the *London A-Z*. It is part of the London Borough of Waltham Forest which also includes the areas of Walthamstow, Leyton and Leytonstone. Former Members of Parliament include Norman Tebbit who was prominent in Margaret Thatcher's administrations of the 1980s, and none other than Winston Churchill when Chingford was in the Epping constituency.

Following Chingford, the next office to open was Chesterton on the outskirts of Cambridge and, four years later, Norwich, in 1982.

In 1986 Price Bailey opened an office in Black Bear Court, Newmarket. Newmarket was 15 miles north-east of Cambridge, effectively on the A11 road to Norwich. The town is, of course, best known for its association with horse racing which dates back to 1174. However, it was King James I, who reigned from 1603 to 1625, who greatly increased the popularity of horse racing at Newmarket. The royal association continued with Charles I inaugurating the first cup race. The present Queen opened The National Stud, a breeding centre for thoroughbred horses, in Newmarket in 1967. With a population of 15,000 it has been calculated that one in three jobs in the town is dependent on horse racing in some way.

In 1990 Price Bailey opened an office in Walsingham chambers in Ely (see Chapter 6).

3 | The Swinging Sixties

WHAT A DECADE!
WE WORKED SATURDAY MORNINGS

WHAT A DECADE!

What was Britain, Great Britain or even the United Kingdom doing in the 1960s? It was doing three things. Socially, it was breaking out from the class and age straitjacket of the 1950s or even, if you like, of the Victorian era. Politically, it was about to try a new form of government, having grown tired of the old Conservative regime which it saw as increasingly incompetent and complacent. Economically, it was waking up to the fact that the world was suddenly a competitive place.

First, socially it was an era of personal liberation or, as Kenneth O. Morgan put it in the book, *From Blitz to Blair*.

In the view of some critics one of moral anarchy. The popular consumer culture of the Beatles, Mary Quant and Carnaby Street was allied to the sexual freedom provided by the pill. The Wilson years were seen by the world as a time of 'permissiveness', no doubt with exaggeration (after all, only nine per cent of single women took the pill in 1970). The children of the post-war baby-boomers trampled over the remains of Victorian puritanism and inhibition. Working-class young people in full employment embraced the pop music and fashion of the new consumerism. The middle-class young went to university on full grants, often in a new mood of rebellious liberation. The anguished response of the critics like Mrs Mary Whitehouse suggested that Britain faced a cultural crisis. In an age of relativism, its moral climate would never be the same.

The government did not create the mood of libertarianism. But it did try to respond to it as best it could, without losing touch with the respectable conservatism of the silent majority. The main legislative response came during, and in part from, Roy Jenkins's time at the Home Office between 1965 and 1967. During this period, the old censorship of the Lord Chamberlain and others over the arts, symbolised in the Crown's prosecution of the publishers of Lady Chatterley's Lover back in 1959, disappeared, with Roy Jenkins presiding over their eclipse like a liberal crusader. The Lord Chamberlain's last gasp came with his censoring of Edward Bond's play Early Morning in 1967 for depicting a lesbian Queen Victoria. Other kinds of freedom were also given tacit encouragement. Homosexuals, the victims of intolerance and persecution since the days of Oscar Wilde, won partial liberation in 1967. A private member's bill, moved by Leo Abse and supported by almost all Labour members, decriminalised homosexual relations in private by consenting adults. Another private member's bill by the Liberal David Steel to allow the abortion of unwanted pregnancies also went through. It was greeted with dismay by the Roman Catholic Church, for which it was clearly a severe defeat. In 1969 the government allowed amendment of the divorce laws, which many had long seen as intrusive and inhuman. It also supported penal reform in decisive fashion. Sydney Silverman's bill for ending capital punishment was passed in 1965; the change was made permanent under Callaghan in 1969. The Wilson years therefore saw a disappearance of the brutality of the rope from British history.

These were freedoms that ended persecution or repression. The government also tried to respond in more positive fashion. Its idealism needs to be remembered as a major feature of the Wilson years. The setting up of a Ministry of Arts, under the inspired choice of Jennie Lee, meant a huge boost for culture, including the funding of the Arts Council, and the British Film Institute. It was a distinguished period for British theatre, for example through the National Theatre Company. London boasted five major orchestras of world renown, while elsewhere orchestras in Manchester, Birmingham and Bournemouth, along with the vitality of opera companies such as the Welsh National Opera, testified to the international pre-eminence of classical British music-making.

It is not possible to write about Britain in the 1960s without mentioning the Beatles and the transformation that they represented. From the Cavern in Liverpool, a wonderful city in the nineteenth century but not greatly admired by the 1960s, the Beatles broke on to the national and indeed, the international stage in 1963. Arthur Marwick in his book, *The Sixties*, put it well, writing:

A year of hit records and television appearances in Britain, together with a performance at *Sunday Night at the London Palladium* on 13 October 1963, led to the emergence of 'Beatlemania' among the group's adoring pre-teen and teenage fans. The Beatles' conquest of Great Britain was ratified by their appearance at a Royal Command Performance at the Prince of Wales Theatre, London. The sight of screaming fans, and the Beatles themselves, telegenic and always ready with

The Beatles – the iconic pop group of the 'swinging sixties'.

laconic and wittily debunking remarks, delivered in broad Liverpudlian accents, became one of the early sixties 'spectacles' …

… There is no point in pretending that the Beatles captivate everyone; but their significance was acknowledged by pretty well everybody who paid attention to the news, and within their own constituency they topped the polls, perhaps in part because they still had the power to annoy the staid and middle-aged.

Politically, it was the turn of the Labour Party to govern the country. The populist newspaper, the *Sun,* showed what it felt was the mood of the voters when it publicised these quotes in the run-up to the 1964 General Election:

Why I am voting Labour

Voter 1: Because I believe a vast amount of talent and energy, especially among the young, will be released if we give Labour a chance to make a new Britain.

Voter 2: Britain of the future shall be a classless one where all petty snobbisms of accent, dress, education will be defunct … a society which seeks to harness the talents of all in the best possible manner.

Dave Lawrence, captain of the winning Bishop's Stortford side,
is carried by his team-mates after their victory in the last Amateur cup final at Wembley in 1974.

Labour's new leader, Harold Wilson, had addressed his party's annual conference in October a year earlier and concluded that Socialism should be recast 'in terms of scientific revolution':

> But that revolution cannot become a reality unless we are prepared to make far-reaching changes in economic and social attitudes which permeate our whole system of society.
>
> The Britain that is going to be forged in the white heat of this revolution will be no place for restrictive practices or for outdated methods on either side of industry …
>
> In the Cabinet and the boardroom alike, those charged with the control of our affairs must be ready to think and speak in the language of our scientific age.

It caught the mood of the moment.

Labour won the 1964 General Election defeating a tired Tory party led by Sir Alec Douglas Home who frightened many voters by admitting that he tackled economic questions counting matches in his hand. With his estate in Scotland he certainly reminded voters of his privileged background far removed from the housing estates in which most of them lived.

The mood of the country was vividly caught by Dominic Sandbrook in his book *White Heat*:

As the endless references to VE Night, the Coronation and even the relief of Mafeking made clear, England's triumph in the World Cup was invested by the press with exaggerated historical significance. By seeing off the French and the Germans, England had supposedly reversed years of decline to plant her foot once again on top of the world. 'Everyone now looks to England to lead the world', the FA secretary said proudly. According to the Sunday Express,

A blaze of Union Jacks waved, as people unashamedly gripped by emotion and patriotism danced, wept and hugged each other ... What they will tell their grandchildren in the years to come is that it was English nerve and English heart and English stamina which finally overcame the tenacious resistance of [West Germany] ... No one who saw this historic World Cup Final can deny England their 'finest hour'.

WE WORKED SATURDAY MORNINGS

Back at Price Bailey, in May 1964 Vernon Clarke was elected a partner and the Agreement drawn up by Wm Gee and Sons of 14 Water Lane, Bishop's Stortford, still had three different names for their offices as it read:

The parties here to [Stanley Price, Reginald Ernest Edward William Bailey, Stanley John Trow and Vernon David Clarke] do hereby severally covenant with each other that they will become and be partners in the profession of Accountants in continuation of the business carried on by Mr Price, Mr Bailey and Mr Trow under the styles of 'Benten, Price and Bailey' at The Guild House Bishop's Stortford in the County of Hertford, 'Price and Bailey' at Aylmer House Harlow in the County of Essex and 'R.E. Bailey and Son' at 2 Glisson Road in the Town and County of Cambridge.

The Agreement went on to say:

(i)   The capital of the firm shall be such sum as the Partners shall from time to time agree to contribute

(ii)   Each Partner shall be entitled to the capital from time to time contributed by him and standing to his credit in the books of the firm.

(iii) Each Partner shall be entitled to interest at the rate of Ten per cent per annum on the amount of capital for the time being standing to his credit in the books of the firm and such interest shall be paid or credited before any division of profits is made

(i)   Mr Price and Mr Bailey shall be entitled to a salary of Three thousand pounds per annum each and Mr Trow and Mr Clarke shall be entitled to a salary of Two thousand two hundred pounds per annum each

(ii)   In ascertaining the profits of the firm each Partner shall be required to account for the value of any personal audit fees directors fees secretarys fees and other remuneration from any client of the practice received by him

The profits of the business after providing for interest and salaries shall belong as to Forty five per cent thereof to Mr Price as to Twenty five per cent thereof to Mr Bailey as to Twenty per cent thereof to Mr Trow and as to Ten per cent thereof to Mr Clarke and they shall respectively bear in the same proportions all losses arising in connection with the said business.

Another long-serving partner of Price Bailey was Andrew Hulme who joined just after Graham Hardy. This is what he said of the firm in the 1960s:

I joined in 1963 having completed a Business Studies Course at Cambridge College of Arts and Technology ('The Tech'). I was interviewed by Reg Bailey one Saturday morning, started for a couple of weeks on 13 July 1963, had four weeks off for pre-arranged holiday, and started 'in earnest' after that at the beginning of September. Starting salary was £3.10s.0d per week with a rise of £1 per week after the first year promised at the outset – no talk of inflation!

We worked Saturday mornings on a rota basis in those days – with some of the staff in one week and the rest in other weeks (I think we did 'one in three')

I took articles in December that year, and at the tender age of 18 was not full capacity to make a contract … so the contract was between Reg Bailey and my father, with me as the 'third party'.

Richard Price who followed his father, Stanley Price, into the firm.

All study costs were borne by me, no contribution from the firm, the usual H. Foulkes-Lynch correspondence course. No full time study but we had (home) study leave prior to each exam of 21 weeks total in the term of our articles

I worked at the Glisson Road Office and the Bradwells Court Office after we moved there but moved on to Bishop's Stortford around 1967 where I joined Stanley Price's team – a sort of precursor to the Audit/Corporate teams of today. We were in the Guild House at that stage. I qualified in 1970 in that team, but was approached later to move to Vernon Clarke's team (today's equivalent would be the Business team). We were short of space in the Guild House and initially I worked in an offshoot office on the High Street at Bishop's Stortford on the first floor above a shop. We only used it for internal working and there were four or five of us there. If I needed to see clients I met them in the Guild House.

On occasions whilst still at Cambridge I had been lent to the Bishop's Stortford office and travelled across with Reg in his Rover – I can't remember what if anything we talked about but they must have been strange trips with a VERY senior partner and a VERY junior clerk travelling together. I do remember, however, that Reg used to go to the Water House restaurant for lunch and took me too when I was on those secondments to Bishop's Stortford.

Later we took on the Water House in Water Lane (previously the Water Lane restaurant) and I worked there, still with Vernon as his manager and a team including Mike Nicholls who was appointed to partnership (actually a profit sharing manager as he could not be a partner under ICAEW rules).

During my time with Vernon the firm took on H.P. Board in Cambridge (see below). And Vernon told me of an opportunity to move back to Cambridge but I had not long been in his team and he was keen not to lose me. Vernon had delayed telling me and by the time I had managed to speak with Reg Bailey about what would be involved he had assumed (wrongly) I was not keen and Roger Evans (then at Bishop's Stortford) had been asked to move to Cambridge.

In 1970 I was in the first batch EVER of staff to have a firm's car – a brand new Morris 1100 two door! The car was OUR 226H and with my daily commute – together with cross ply tyres and 3000-mile service intervals the garage did quite well – a set of tyres every nine months and three or four services a year!

In 1974 Vernon and Stanley asked me to go to lunch with them and told me that, following Tom Parkin's death, I could move to Harlow with a view to an early partnership. I was told in no uncertain terms that I had to move to the area. Whilst working at BS I had been travelling daily from my parents' home near Cambridge. The office administrator was able to arrange for a Council flat in Harlow with the Development Corporation ('key employee moving into the area'). Partnership was from 1 June 1975 (firm's year end at that point was 31 May). I was offered partnership with the then terms of ten years to parity! Holidays improved over my manager position and but not the full 7 weeks – that was to come later in the build-up to parity (I think after three years at five weeks – but in those days that was generous, so no complaints). My salary as a partner at that time was £3000 pa (£60,000 in today's money) and I drew in my first year as partner the £3000 as drawings, ie what I had been having gross was now my annual drawings with tax to be sorted on profits … and at that rate I was quite comfortable!

I was less than delighted with the town and for some while spent a limited amount of time there – three or four nights in the flat, and with a social life in and around Cambridge spent weekends and some midweek nights at my parents' house. I joined the Rotary Club in Harlow but it was difficult to be keen when their activities were in Harlow at the weekends – when I wanted to be flying with the Gliding Club near Cambridge!

In due course I bought a flat in Sawbridgeworth which was much better, and began to spend more time in the area.

About Price Bailey's offices, Andrew Hulme said:

Cambridge had been officially opened at Reg Bailey's home, but so far I guess no work was being done there – it was just a Cambridge address for the firm. When I joined in 1963 we were over an Insurance broker at 2 Glisson Road – in a three or four room complex – coffee, by the way was made by me at 10.30, tea at 3.30 and that was it, none of these constant visits to the coffee room.

We moved to Bradwells Court in three of four rooms on top of PolyTravel and it was while we were there that I moved off to Bishop's Stortford. However we were still working on Saturday mornings and we came to an arrangement that meant I worked my Saturdays at Cambridge to help them staff the office and save me travelling to Bishop's Stortford just for a morning.

Then in the late 1970s the firm took over H.P. Board & Son in Cintra House and moved into their offices.

And on the firm's cars he said:

The firm had partner cars when I joined in 1963. Reg Bailey was running a Vauxhall Victor at the time and later updated to a rather posh maroon Rover 90. The first managers to be offered cars in 1970 were Mike Nicholls, Tony Saban and I think Graham Savage and Mike Harwood and I were offered cars. I was asked 'if I had the choice what would I have' – I said Morris 1100 and Hunts garage (client at Bishop's Stortford) supplied it. The others had Vauxhall Vivas from Franklins Garage – also a Bishop's Stortford client.

4 | Growth continues

ACQUIRING MORE PRACTICES
ABACUS
VAT

ACQUIRING MORE PRACTICES

The 1970s was a difficult decade for economies across the world, not least the UK's. The rate of inflation had started to accelerate in the 1960s as successive governments set about achieving full employment. Determined to avoid a return to the high unemployment levels of the 1930s, successive governments (both Labour and Conservative) implemented Keynesian policies to keep demand high, using public money to prime the economy pump. The result, in a Britain with some archaic industrial management and workforce practices, was the creation of greater demand than supply – the classic cause of inflation.

However, this was just a foretaste of what was to come in the 1970s. Anthony Barber, the Chancellor of the Exchequer in Heath's government, pumped money into the economy as never before in 1971 and 1972 following the news that unemployment had broken through the one million barrier, a shocking total following 30 years of full employment. Unfortunately, Britain's expansion coincided with a world boom, sparked by the decision in the United States to print money rather than raise taxes, in order to pay for the increasingly expensive involvement in Vietnam. In 1971 the US turned from being an exporter of oil into a net importer; and in October 1973, when yet another Arab-Israeli conflict, the Yom Kippur War, broke out, the Arab oil producers chose the moment to quadruple the price of oil and cut back production. The effect on world trade was little short of disastrous. Both industry and consumers had become extremely profligate in their use of oil, which had been getting cheaper and cheaper in real terms over the previous decade. As panic buying and speculation took hold, the price rocketed. Tens of billions of pounds, dollars, deutschmarks, francs and lire were taken out of the world economy and put in the Arabian Desert. Until they could be recycled into the system, the world was going to suffer.

And suffer it did, as Britain with its continuing structural weakness suffered more than most. The Barber Boom had not worked. British manufacturers had not invested as much as had been hoped, and the two main results of the expansion in credit had been an explosion in property prices and a rapid increase in inflation. Resentment grew among workers, who benefited little from the rising property and stock market prices but felt the impact of rising prices in the shops.

In an attempt to choke inflation, Heath's government tackled the symptoms – rising prices, dividends and earnings – without tackling the cause: too much money. In the autumn of 1973, just before the oil crisis, the government introduced stage one of an incomes policy which would allow index-linked rises if inflation rose above 7 per cent. Because of the oil-price hike, inflation rose quickly above that level and the automatic pay rises gave a ratchet effect pushing it higher and higher.

The National Union of Mineworkers submitted a large claim and imposed an overtime ban on 8 November 1973. Heath panicked and declared a state of emergency on 13 November. A month later he declared a three-day week to preserve fuel, and though negotiations with both Arabs and the miners continued, the only results were the continuation of high oil prices and the actuality of a miners' strike rather than just the threat. In the end, and for some people three weeks too late, Heath called an election with the implied platform of: 'Who governs the country, the government or the unions?' The electorate decided it wasn't sure who should govern the country. The Tories had finally shown some signs of standing up to the unions, but Labour might get the miners back to work. Neither party gained an overall majority, but Labour came away with more seats. Heath tried unsuccessfully to negotiate a coalition with the Liberal Democrats, so Harold Wilson formed his third administration.

The Labour government gave in to the NUM and when the rest of the unions followed in the headlong rush, inflation soared to 25 per cent. While inflation was soaring and everyone tried to keep pace, financial institutions, and to a lesser extent manufacturing businesses, were suffering severely from the financial squeeze that had finally been imposed in the autumn of 1973. Nearly all the secondary banks went into liquidation or, if it was deemed necessary to maintain confidence, were rescued by the main banks promoted by the Bank of England. If the new Chancellor, Denis Healey, had not introduced a corporate tax-saving measure, stock relief, many manufacturing companies would have failed. On the Stock Exchange, prices fell throughout 1974 and the Financial Times 30-share index reached 147 in early January 1975 (having been over 150 as long ago as 1946).

By 1975 inflation was starting to have a serious effect not only on those who had retired and those without the protection of powerful unions, but on British industry in general.

International confidence in the British government collapsed completely when Labour's 1976 party conference championed the nationalisation of the leading high-street banks and the largest insurance companies. In the autumn of 1976 sterling began to fall like a stone.

The Chancellor of the Exchequer, Denis Healey, was forced to make a humiliating return from Heathrow airport on his way to an International Monetary Fund conference in Manila. Instead of going to Manila, Healey went to the Labour party conference in Blackpool, where the new Prime Minister, James Callaghan (Harold Wilson had resigned in the spring of 1976), had already made a blunt speech to the delegates:

> Britain has lived too long on borrowed time, borrowed money, borrowed ideas …
> For too long, perhaps ever since the war, we've postponed facing up to fundamental changes in our society and our economy. That is what I mean when I say we have been living on borrowed time. For too long this country, all of us – yes, this conference too – has been ready to settle for borrowing money abroad to maintain our standards of life, instead of grappling with the fundamental problems of British industry.
>
> We used to think that you could spend your way out of a recession and increase employment by cutting taxes and boosting government spending.

Meanwhile, there were several developments on the Price Bailey front in the 1970s and this is how Graham Hardy remembered them:

> After Tom's death Andrew Hulme moved from Cambridge to Harlow and became a partner in 1975. At the same time Peter Bass who had worked with me in Harlow for several years became a profit sharing manager. Peter was a certified accountant and at that time could not be a partner. However he was regarded as partner equivalent as were Michael Nicholls at Bishops Stortford and Tony Saban at Cambridge who became managers at the same time. 1975 was a year for big changes as in addition to all these appointments Richard Price and Nigel Bailey were also made partners.
>
> Richard was Stanley's son and had trained with a firm in London, although he was not yet qualified. He began with the firm at Harlow and I always felt that he had a most difficult job as a partner's son, to be accepted by the staff until he qualified, which he did a few months after joining us. [Richard Price recalled that he found things difficult in the Harlow office where Price Bailey acted mostly for sole traders. Later, in the 1970s, the firm expanded in the town.] He moved to Bishop's Stortford in 1969 where I felt he would progress better.

Nigel Bailey was Reginald's nephew and he had also joined us after training but before qualifying a few years before. In 1972 we had opened an office in Dunmow and he had moved there to be manager, being linked to the Bishops Stortford office. At the time with communications and road transport not being as they are now he was trusted to sign all cheques from that office on his own. We maintained a client account as well as an office account. This was mainly used for the purpose of receiving tax refunds and paying them over the clients, but Nigel had also received larger sums of money from some clients for investment.

Stanley Price telephoned me one Monday afternoon to say that Richard had been to see Nigel and challenged him about client money and he had confessed to taking about £15,000 of it for own purposes. This resulted in his suspension and the removal of all relevant papers to the basement of the Water House in Bishops Stortford. All partners met there on the Sunday morning to try and find out the true extent of the problem. It was decided that I would take over the calculation of what was missing which I did over the next five weeks working full time in the basement. A subsequent tenant of the Water House told me that a local ghost, the Grey Lady of Bishop Stortford, had been seen in the basement. I was very glad that I did not know that at the time!

The eventual outcome of my work showed that Nigel had misappropriated over £100,000 [about £800,000 in today's money] of client money. He eventually admitted this and had of course been dismissed from the firm. We were fortunate in that apart from the excess our professional indemnity insurance policy refunded all the losses to our clients. Michael Horwood took on the task of contacting all the clients who had been affected, which was probably a more difficult job than the one I had.

We were worried as to how our reputation would be affected especially as the subsequent court case was reported locally. However, any client who had lost money was recompensed in full and we managed to weather the storm without too much damage.

As we shall see, Price Bailey was not affected too adversely by this unfortunate behaviour by one of its partners and Graham Hardy went on to say:

Fortunately on the departure of Nigel we already had Peter Gillman at the Dunmow office and he was able to take over the responsibility for the management of that office before becoming a partner in 1982 to coincide with the retirement of Stanley Price and Reginald Bailey. Peter had been articled to me at

Harlow and I remember him attending his interview proudly wearing a badge saying 'Deputy Head Boy'.

Peter soon progressed well and was moved to Dunmow before he qualified. As we know, Peter eventually became Managing Partner and then Managing Director on the firm becoming a Limited Liability Partnership where he has been enormously successful. It is a matter of some pride to me that he was articled to me.

Meanwhile, on 20 May 1970 Graham Savage and Michael Horwood were elected partners of Price Bailey & Partners, and, in March 1972, Richard Price was asked by the partners to be responsible for administration of the Audit Department. In February 1974 it was announced that on 1 June 1974 Nigel Bailey, Roger Evans and Richard Price would be admitted to the partnership. At the same time, the managers Mike Nicholls, Geoffrey Roberts and Anthony Saban, while not becoming partners, would be granted equivalent status.

Expansion during the 1970s was not without some teething problems as this 'NOTICE TO ALL STAFF' from Stanley Price in September 1976 shows:

The Partners again remind all staff that the present method of providing free drinks is on the basis of one drink mid-morning and one drink mid-afternoon for staff working in the office. Despite previous warning this facility is still being abused involving a considerable waste of time. The Partners therefore give notice that unless this abuse stops forthwith the supply of free drinks will cease.

Whilst we have no wish to prevent staff receiving or making emergency telephone calls, far too much time is spent by many, receiving and making private telephone calls, often occupying lines so that clients complain of the difficulty in calling the office. This also must cease.

ABACUS

On 15 February 1982, Price Bailey launched a staff magazine. It was called ABACUS and consisted of two pages (printed both sides) in black and white and stapled together. (This was the height, or rather depth, of the early 1980s recession.)

Ian Smith, in the Bishop's Stortford office, was heavily involved. The magazine continued quarterly until the end of 1984.

ABACUS

Issue No. 8   December 1984

EDITORIAL

I must apologise again for the fact that there has **not** been an issue of Abacus since last April. (In fact, you'll be lucky if you even get this one by Christmas!)

As most of you know, Janet Buttery, your editor of Abacus for the past 18 months or so, recently left Price, Bailey and Partners to take up a position in a different field as Clerk to Stansted Parish Council. I am sure everybody will join me in wishing her all the best for the future.

On a serious note, if we are to continue producing Abacus, may I reiterate the importance of everybody doing their best to send in contributions for inclusion in the newsletter. Perhaps each office could appoint someone to report any news to me (engagements, marriages, exam successes, etc.) and to chase people up to do a bit of writing or to send in a joke or two; anything (or nearly anything!) will be accepted.

Easter next year is early in April, so that would be a good time for the next issue. So, come on everyone, get those articles flooding in.

Thank you.

Wendy Fleckney.

In 1982 Price Bailey launched a staff magazine and called it ABACUS.

I'm not at my best in the morning,
I'm not one to rise with the lark,
I'm not one to welcome each dawning —
More a night owl who shines after dark.
It's due to my habits nocturnal
That the early birds drive me insane
As I flex every muscle in turn, then
Yawn — and go back to sleep again.

CHRISTMAS COCKTAILS

Dotted about in this issue you will find a few recipes for exciting cocktails. Why not try them out at Christmas, but don't go too mad!

FLAMING FIZZ

1 sugar cube, rubbed over zest of an orange; 1 tbsp. brandy; top up with sparkling wine.

GLASGOW GURGLE

1 tbsp. whisky; top up with stout.

'Was there anything else apart from my return being incorrect and late?'

Ian Smith joined Price Bailey in 1971 and is still there after 40 years.

Alan Philips, another long-serving member of the Price Bailey team. He joined the firm on 1 June 1967, two months before the present Managing Director was born!

VAT

An important development, both for British business and therefore accountancy practices, was the introduction of Value Added Tax, or VAT, as it quickly became known.

It was introduced in 1973 by Chancellor of the Exchequer, Anthony Barber, in Edward Heath's Conservative Government in power from June 1970 to February 1974. It replaced a sales tax called Purchase Tax and initially was levied at 10 per cent. Since then it has gradually risen and is currently 20 per cent with lower rates for some goods and services and complete exemptions for others such as books and exports.

The arguments in favour are that it is a tax on consumption and expenditure rather than income and that is simpler to collect than a sales tax. Some critics consider it a regressive tax meaning that the poor pay more as a percentage of their income than the rich. Defenders argue that relating taxation to income is arbitrary and the VAT is a proportional tax and that those with a higher income consume more and therefore pay more tax.

There is no doubt that it was a development that businesses needed to understand and implement properly because they effectively became the tax collector

Partners in Price Bailey in the 1980s. L to R: Roger Evans, Vernon Clarke, John Riseborough, Graham Hardy and Mike Nicholls.

for the government. They had to make a return to HM Revenue and Customs either monthly or quarterly and pay whatever was due from sales they had made less VAT they had been charged by their suppliers. Only businesses with an annual income lower than a certain level (currently £79,000) were exempt.

Certain businesses, such as publishers, did not charge their customers VAT as books were exempt but could reclaim the VAT charged by suppliers. HM Revenue and Customs gradually realised that this situation was open to abuse in that businesses could start up, claim rebates for two or three years and then close down. As a result, whereas HM Revenue and Customs used to try and make inspections of *all* businesses every three or four years, they now tend to concentrate on those making claims or those where the returns are erratic.

An example is one of Price Bailey's clients in Cambridge, Icon Books Ltd, which began trading in 1992. It made its VAT returns, making claims, every quarter and, as it grew quite quickly, the claims became quite substantial. As a result, HMRC made an inspection every year from 1992 to 1996. Nothing was ever found to be awry and finally, Martin Clapson, who handled the Icon account, said to the local VAT inspector:

Punting on the Cam past Queens' College, Cambridge. (Works in Print/Don McCrae)

'Look, you have inspected this company five times in the last five years. Price Bailey monitors its VAT returns and you have never found any mistakes. Each inspection costs our client money. Do you think you could trust us to make honest returns?'

The Revenue complied and the company did not have another inspection for 14 years when again, it showed a clean bill-of-health.

Nevertheless, companies were capable, wittingly or unwittingly, of making errors and, in 1989, Price Bailey appointed a VAT specialist, Bob McLachlan, to operate a VAT health service check and extend the firm's existing consultancy service. In a Press Release sent to all clients in November 1989 they said:

Formerly employed by HM Customs and Excise, with wide experience in the control of VAT, Bob's function is to ensure that timely advice to clients will prevent additional liabilities arising.

Tax payers registered for VAT purposes can expect routine control visits by inspectors. These visits could be a source of further costly investigations and penalties where discrepancies are discovered. So a timely VAT health check can prove extremely valuable.

As Bob says: 'There were 460,000 routine visits by Customs and Excise to taxpayers in the year ended 31st March 1989. These visits revealed that additional VAT of £847M was due from taxpayers and over-declarations of £24M had been made. VAT health checks by Price Bailey could well have discovered these irregularities at an earlier stage. They will help to avoid the worry that a prolonged VAT investigation can cause and will save penalties being imposed by Customs and Excise.

5 | The move into Norfolk

A THRIVING COMMUNITY
NEED TO BE IN CITY CENTRE
AMBITIOUS PLANS

A THRIVING COMMUNITY

Opening an office in Norwich was a big development for Price Bailey. First, although it stuck to the A11 rule, indeed, Norwich is the end of the A11, it was a considerable distance from Bishop's Stortford which, at the time, was effectively the Head Office of the firm. Second, Norwich, with a population of 174,000, was a much bigger conurbation than any other Price Bailey location.

In the fifteenth and sixteenth centuries Norwich was a wealthy and important city. For example both Henry V and Henry VIII borrowed money from bankers in the city to finance their adventures in France. And in the late seventeenth and throughout the eighteenth centuries Norwich was a formidable force in the cloth industry comparable with Yorkshire and the West Country. However, as K.J. Allison wrote in *Norwich and its Region*:

> Norwich was faced by mounting competition from foreign and home-made cloths, above all from West Riding worsteds. The lower-grade types were soon extensively made in Yorkshire, and it was only the finest stuffs which enabled Norfolk to compete with considerable success for so long. The West Riding's advantages are well known. It was Yorkshire sheep and Yorkshire spinners that provided Norwich with much of its wool and yarn. It was Leeds and Bradford, not Norwich, that had local water-power, coal and iron with which to share in the Industrial Revolution. It was Yorkshiremen, not Norfolkmen, who adventurously experimented with machinery. By the middle of the nineteenth century the Norfolk industry was almost dead.

Fortunately, other industries survived and prospered, most notably the boot and shoe industry which employed 28,700 people in the area in 1931 compared with just over 4,000 in 1851. Those in metal, wood and electrical employment grew from 2,000 to 5,000 and in food and drink from fewer than 1,000 to nearly

Norwich Cathedral. (Works in Print/Richard Osbourne)

5,000 in the same period. In the food area, the milling firm of J. and J. Colman, eventually part of Reckitt & Colman, was very important. Established in 1804 at nearby Stoke Moll Cross, Colmans moved to Carrow Works in Norwich in 1856. Manufacturing mustard and starch, by 1900 they alone employed 2,200 people.

In the later twentieth century Norwich continued as a strong manufacturing centre with Start-rite shoes, Boulton & Paul, the structural steel works manufacturers, Barnards, the inventors of machine-produced wire netting, and electrical engineers Lawrence Scott and Electromotors. It also had a long association with chocolate manufacture through Caley's, taken over by Mackintosh who merged with Rowntree and were then taken over by Nestlé who moved production to York. Jarrolds, printer and publisher, founded in 1810, was an important employer and is now best known as the owner of the only independent department store in the city. There were also a number of brewers though most were taken over and no significant brewery is left. Finally, there was insurance. Norwich Union grew from an amalgamation of various insurance companies and by the 1930s was employing 1,300 people in the city.

The Second World War had a profound effect on Norwich's manufacturing. Much of its capacity was diverted to military requirements while many of the employees were called into the armed services with the boot and shoe industry alone losing 3,000 workers. Moreover, Norwich was heavily bombed and many of its factories were either destroyed or badly damaged.

The post-war period brought recovery as it did everywhere else and both Norwich's manufacturing and services grew again. By the time Price Bailey looked at opening an office in the city in the early 1980s Norwich was a thriving community with a healthy balance of manufacturing and service industries and surrounded by countryside with many prosperous farms.

The move into Norwich took the form of a takeover of the established practice of Graver, Madders & Co. which consisted of Miss Graver, Miss Madders and four staff, one of whom, Janice Bowthorpe, a secretary, is still working for the firm in 2012. The offices were in a terraced house in Old Palace Road which was about a mile from the city centre and could best be described as a somewhat run-down area. On one side of the office was a junk shop and on the other an empty house. Price Bailey bought the empty house and linked it to the existing office. The main advantage of the location was that clients could at least park outside without having to struggle with car parks in the city centre.

Miss Graver left within a few months and Miss Madders two years later. Initially, Lawrence Bailey and Roger Evans would make weekly visits and in October 1982 Michael Horwood, a partner in the Bishop's Stortford office, became the resident partner in Norwich. He brought a number of tax clients from Bishop's Stortford and, to help, also brought up the tax manager, John Mills. Mills stayed in Norwich for two years before moving back to Bishop's Stortford. Richard Day, still a partner in the Norwich office, had already joined the firm and, in 1985 both he and John Riseborough, who was recruited from Thompson McLintock, now KPMG, were appointed partners.

This was the announcement Vernon Clarke made to the staff in February 1982:

The partners are pleased to announce that as from 1st March 1982 we will be acquiring the accountancy practice of Graver, Madders & Co. in Norwich.

Miss Graver will be continuing as a Consultant and Miss Madder will be a local partner of Price, Bailey and Partners.

As from 1st March Roger Clarke of our Cambridge Office will transfer to Norwich as Manager.

Roger Evans and Lawrence Bailey will supervise the Norwich Office from Cambridge and Andrew Hulme will spend approximately two days a week in Cambridge in anticipation of transferring to Cambridge full time on the retirement of Mr. Reginald Bailey on 31st May.

This was followed in September 1982 by:

To assist with the growth of our Norwich Practice Mr. Michael Horwood will be moving to the Norwich Office early in the New Year. Mr. John Mills will also be moving to the Norwich Office.

From the beginning of October until Mr. Horwood's transfer is complete Mr. Norman Hall will be assisting at Norwich.

Mr. Ian Smith is to take charge of the Tax Department.

NEED TO BE IN CITY CENTRE

It was soon clear that Price Bailey needed to move to the city centre to show the local business community, including the banks, that the firm was a serious player in the accountancy business. The Graver Madders clients had been largely sole traders, mainly shopkeepers and subcontractors. In March 1985 the office was moved to Horse Fair House, initially called Provincial House. It also had on-site parking which was considered essential if existing clients were to be retained.

In 1987 Price Bailey took over Norfolk and Norwich Accountancy Services. Their clients were mostly small businesses as well but these included several of the smaller firms of solicitors who would prove to be good contacts. Along with contacts from banks, Price Bailey were soon signing up new and larger clients. The practice grew steadily and needed to take on more offices opposite Horse Fair House, where they were only occupying the front wing. They were able to move back when Lloyds bank moved out of the back.

In the 1990s, John Riseborough, who became the managing partner of the Norwich office, and eventually of the whole Price Bailey group, was determined to make the firm more than just the 'boring accountants'. He said in October 2001:

Clients often comment on the fact that we don't fit the stereotype. We are

*John Riseborough joined Price Bailey from Thompson McLintock,
now KPMG, to run the Norwich office.*

passionate about what we do, pragmatic in the way we do it and the results speak for themselves.

He felt that Price Bailey was one of the first regional firms to recognise the need to broaden its services away from traditional regulatory work, and has very successfully diversified into non-traditional areas. He added:

We have seen a definite shift in the kind of services that businesses require from us. We are no longer just accountants in the traditional sense. Instead we see ourselves primarily as business advisers, playing a much wider role in helping our clients achieve their strategic goals.

The extra services included:

- Business consultancy – including strategic planning and profit improvement for businesses, together with financial management.

- Corporate finance – during the past 12 months alone, the firm's practice-wide corporate finance team has advised on MBOs, acquisitions and capital investment deals totalling more than £100 million.

- Forensic accounting – investigating and analysing detailed financial 'evidence' which can then be used to pursue or defend legal actions relating to, for example, commercial disputes or personal injury claims.

- IT consultancy – services range from hardware installation to the creation of bespoke software packages, and often involve the design and implementation of comprehensive management information systems.

- People management – including management recruitment, team appraisals, management development training and the design and implementation of structured pay and bonus schemes.

- Financial Services – expert, impartial advice on employee benefits, personal pensions and investments.

Riseborough added:

We are very aware of the need to provide depth as well as breadth of services. Our firm-wide commitment to training and development has enabled us to achieve very high levels of in-house expertise in all these areas, while helping us to attract new staff of the highest calibre. The term 'specialisms' is often over-used – but when we say it, we mean it.

By 2003, when it was celebrating 21 years in Norwich, Price Bailey was able to show how well it had done in the city. The *Eastern Daily Press* wrote:

PRICE BAILEY CELEBRATES 21 YEARS IN NORWICH
Price Bailey chartered accountants has been an active part of the Norwich business community for the last 21 years. Today their clients are as diverse as their services and a team of 28 people serves the needs of individuals and small to medium-sized

enterprises (SMEs) throughout the local region. So what has happened to this firm over the past 21 years and what does the future hold?

Price Bailey Chartered Accountants has made huge strides in shedding the old 'boring accountants' image in favour of a reputation for being dynamic and down to earth. 'Clients often comment on the fact that we don't fit the stereotype,' says the Norwich Office managing partner John Riseborough. 'We are passionate about what we do, pragmatic in the way that we do it – and the results speak for themselves'.

Price Bailey established a presence in Norwich 21 years ago when it acquired a small local practice. By 1985 the firm had outgrown its original premises and moved to Horse Fair House in St Faith's Lane which offered a convenient location and onsite parking. Continual growth was enhanced by the acquisition of a

Partners outside the Norwich office.
L to R: Richard Day, Michael Horwood, Colin Long and John Riseborough.

further practice two years later and Price Bailey now occupies the entire first floor of Horse Fair House, having more than doubled its original square footage.

Throughout its 21 years in Norwich, Price Bailey has provided continuity for its clients and more than one third of the team have completed more than 15 years' service – a further testament to their success!

Present – More Than Just Accountants

Price Bailey is now one of the Eastern Region's largest chartered accountancy and business advisory firms, listed number 38 in Accountancy Magazine's Top 60 Accountancy League Table of 2003. With nine offices and more than 200 partners and staff, the firm has developed a strong reputation for providing a breadth as well as a depth of skills.

Price Bailey was one of the UK's first regional accounting firms to recognise that businesses needed a broader range of services from their accountants than the traditional regulatory work. Hence the firm diversified very successfully into areas such as business development, financial services, recruitment, forensic accounting, and specialist VAT and tax consultancy, to name but a few.

Price Bailey's financial services department has become an integral part of the overall package and has recently been set up as a separate business to provide independent financial advice. PB Financial Planning Limited helps individuals plan for their financial future, offering a range of products from investments and pensions through to mortgages and retirement planning.

Future – Creating Precision Business

As for the future, the firm believes that an innovative approach to new services, coupled with a commitment to training and development will enable them to maintain high levels of in-house expertise in all areas, while helping to attract new staff of the highest calibre.

'Providing the best possible service has always been our top priority – and that goes for all our clients, whatever their size', explains John Riseborough. 'We can ensure our clients receive the kind of efficient, personal service they deserve, from people who really understand their business needs.'

AMBITIOUS PLANS

In 2006 Price Bailey moved to much larger premises on St Andrew's Business Park in Thorpe on the outskirts of the city. By this time there were 30 staff and they filled the 3,000 square feet the firm had taken on the first floor. This was

Her Majesty the Queen on an official visit to Norwich.

part of the whole Price Bailey strategy of upgrading the quality of their offices while relocating away from city centres. As the move was made, Peter Gillman, the Managing Director, said:

> We certainly have very ambitious plans for our Norwich office and there is considerable scope for growth. The Norfolk economy is buoyant, the other harbour scheme at Yarmouth is progressing and Norwich International Airport is seeing rapid expansion.

In 2010 the Norwich office made another leap forward when it made a partial acquisition of Quinney & Co. The *Eastern Daily Press* wrote, under the heading:

Delia Smith supporting the Norwich City football team.

Another partner acquired by firm

Regional accountancy firm Price Bailey has just acquired a large part of another local accountancy practice for an undisclosed sum, adding a fourth partner to its Norwich office. The move will mean Price Bailey has doubled the number of its partners it has in its Norwich office from two to four in the past month.

It has also taken on a director, manager and clients, who will all move over to the Norwich office, through the part acquisition of Reepham firm, Quinney & Co.

The staff will move over to Price Bailey's Norwich office. Quinney & Co. will also continue to be run by its founder, Bill Quinney, who retains his clients along with seven staff.

John Warren joined the Norwich team as a partner in 2010.

Richard Day, longest serving partner at Price Bailey's Norwich office, said the move was part of an aggressive growth strategy. He said the firm was aiming to double in size in Norwich in the next two to three years.

'We are looking to recruit other members of staff, our aim is to double the size of the office in two or three years' time.

'The practice recognises that the Norfolk marketplace is quite unique, and by inviting established local practitioners to join our office here, we believe that we can service our clients to the highest standards, and ensure that they get value for money.'

Price Bailey opened its Norwich office in 1982 and now has 30 staff in the city.

The new staff are John Warren, who joins as partner within the business team. He specialises in owner-managed businesses.

Bill Lakey joins the private client team as tax director.

His background is developing and delivering tax strategies for businesses and high-net-worth individuals.

Richard French will assist Mr Lakey as tax manager within the private client team.

In the past year, Price Bailey, headquartered in Bishop's Stortford, has grown to 23 partners, and opened a seventh office in Guernsey.

The practice is placed 36 (up one place on last year) in the *Accountancy Age* Top 50 listing for 2010, and employs a total of 225 staff.

6 | 50 years and onwards

EXPANSION IN THE 1980s

The 1980s began for Price Bailey with the retirement in 1982 of Stanley Price and Reg Bailey. This was clearly an important event as they had been responsible for building the success of the firm up to that moment and for putting in place the people to carry on building Price Bailey.

This was Andrew Hulme's memory of the early 1980s:

In the early 1980s we had taken Lawrence Bailey into partnership in Cambridge to provide for his father's retirement. However, by the time that came in 1982, Lawrence was so busy and had done so well in portfolio development that another partner was needed and I grabbed the opportunity of a return to Cambridge by which time the office was at 93 Regent Street. We opened an office in Newmarket, mainly for extra floor space at a reasonable cost, with Ray Fuller as manager.

This is how Graham Hardy saw the Price Bailey expansion from 1979:

In 1979 I was approached by an employee of solicitors who were clients in Aylmer House who asked me to act for her husband's building company. He had used a firm in Chingford but recently after the owner had died his widow had appointed a manager whom she had dismissed after some financial irregularities. The manager turned out to be the same person I had replaced when I first joined the firm!

I felt this might be an opportunity for expansion and contacted the widow to ask if we could help. As a result I visited her and we soon agreed terms for us to take over the practice and our presence in Chingford started. Both Andrew Hulme and Peter Bass were very keen on the acquisition and to my delight agreed to share the supervision of the new office between them. I have to say they made a very good job of it.

(opposite, top)
Reg Bailey and
Stanley Price at
their retirement
party in 1982.

(opposite, bottom)
Partners at the
retirement party.
L to R: Lawrence
Bailey, Peter
Gillman, Roger
Evans, Michael
Horwood, Norman
Hall, Graham
Hardy, Tony Saban,
Mike Nicholls,
Andrew Hulme,
Vernon Clarke, Peter
Bass, Richard Price
and Graham Savage.

(below) A group of
partners and wives at
the retirement party.

Over the next few years we acquired a few more practices and opened offices in Saffron Walden, Haverhill, Norwich, Newmarket, Ely and Chesterton. With the practice growing to this extent the partners decided that we should have an Executive Committee to handle day to day matters and report to partners meetings. Vernon Clarke, who had been at Harlow when I joined the firm and had moved to Bishop's Stortford when he became a partner in 1965 and was now senior partner, was made chairman. He is remembered, amongst other things, for always keeping a radio in his desk drawer so that he could follow the Test Matches. The other members were Roger Evans from the Cambridge office and me.

We were involved in most of the discussions to develop the practice and Roger and I particularly wanted to get things moving more quickly so that partners meetings set out policy and the Executive Committee implemented it. That was the theory but I am not sure if in practice we always stuck to this and some partners became less happy with our roles and began to talk about having a managing partner instead.

To my surprise I was asked to be the first managing partner but I turned the suggestion down three times, because I had one of the largest client portfolios in the firm, had a big commitment to my position at the Harlow and District Sports Trust

and I was far from convinced that all the partners were committed to the role. I was also unsure that I would be the best choice and my vote would have gone to Roger. Vernon had indicated that he wanted to retire and had withdrawn from the Executive, being replaced by John Riseborough from the Norwich office, with whom I later worked closely and very happily. I had a lot of confidence in John's judgement.

Eventually I gave in when Roger was sent to ask me to take up the role and I began it in 1989. I soon found that I was expected to produce the firm's accounts with the help of our Practice Administrator. I had not anticipated this but was keen to do it as I had always prepared management accounts to show the level of chargeable time in each office and their recovery rates as well as profitability. Preparing the firm's accounts gave me an insight into areas I had not dealt with before. The Practice Administrator, whilst having many good qualities, had not taken his accountancy training beyond a semi-senior level and was quite unable to prepare these figures without considerable input from me. This frustrated several of the partners who had their own ideas of how I should be spending my time and administration was not one of them.

In January 1984 Price Bailey appointed Peter Crouch FCA, FCCA, ACIS as their training officer and he was to have a considerable impact over the coming years. He set up a proper training programme and as the current Managing Director, Martin Clapson pointed out, a number of the current partners – Martin himself, Howard Sears, Paul Cullen and Nick Pollington – all went through that programme in the second half of the 1980s and all agreed that they benefited enormously.

Peter Crouch had begun his career in London working for the Inland Revenue and, after qualifying as a chartered accountant, developed a flair for teaching. He moved to a large accounting tuition college, Emile Woolf, and became a director. After six years there he left to help set up a new college, Accountancy Tutors. He was appointed a partner of Price Bailey in July 1989. At the same time, David Robinson was also appointed a partner. He had joined Price Bailey straight from college and had qualified in 1981. His speciality was computer audits and he had been particularly helpful to many clients as he installed computerised accountancy systems.

In the following month Price Bailey announced that it had set up Price Bailey Financial Services Ltd in conjunction with independent advisers, Chapman How Financial Management. The aim of this new company was to offer its clients an expanded range of services to include life insurance, pensions, unit trusts and investment advice.

The Price Bailey office in Newmarket in the 1980s.

The Price Bailey office in Saffron Walden in the 1980s.

David Robinson and Peter Crouch.

Michael Howard became a director of this new company and said:

Traditionally accountants have always advised clients about financial services but have not been able to provide them. Now Price Bailey can do just that.

The company also aimed to offer specialist tax advice enabling clients to organise their finances in the most tax efficient way.

On 29 January 1986 it was announced that new offices would be opened in Newmarket and Saffron Walden. Newmarket would be staffed from the

Paul Cullen spoke highly of Peter Crouch's training in the 1980s.

Cambridge office and Saffron Walden from the Dunmow office. The following year Price Bailey acquired the accountancy practice of Deighton Ruddle and Company of 17 Museum Street, Saffron Walden.

On 31 May 1987, Norman Hall retired and Alasdair MacGillivray was elected a partner.

A LONG AND PROUD HISTORY

The next move came in November 1989 when Price Bailey opened an office in Ely.

Ely itself had a long and proud history. Its origin was the foundation of an abbey in 673 AD. This was destroyed by Danish invaders but a cathedral was built from 1083 onwards. Its octagon is considered 'one of the wonders of the medieval world' and the well-known architectural historian, Nickolaus Pevsner, said it 'is a delight from beginning to end for anyone who feels for space as strongly as for construction and is the greatest individual achievement of architectural genius at Ely Cathedral.'

In his book, *Growing Up in Cambridge, from Austerity to Prosperity,* Alec Forshaw wrote,

Wonderful though King's College Chapel is, forgetting the Rubens, it was outshone in my childish eyes by another, Ely Cathedral. For me this mighty galleon sailing proudly in the wide expanse of the Fens was the greatest wonder. Perhaps it was driving north through Cottenham or Waterbeach up onto the Stretham-Wilburton ridge, and seeing the first glimpse through mist of the serrated outline of the west tower and the octagon, or on clear days the distant views from Newmarket Heath when the sun glinted on stone. In Ely itself the cathedral completely dominates the town, from all directions, and with all its monastic relics, the school, the close, the cloisters, the Bishop's Palace, it was like a town in its own right. To me the cathedral seemed both mysterious and miraculous. Why did the west tower, like a magnified vision of Great St Mary's, not collapse like the Norman crossing tower had done in

1322? How did Alan of Walsingham manage to raise the eight tall tree trunks to form the lantern as the crown of the massive stone octagon? After smashing up the inside of the Lady Chapel, why did Cromwell's iconoclastic troops not carry on and destroy more?

Unlike the unity of King's College, Ely seemed to have many layers of history and different levels of interest, from the stupendous rhythm of the nave arcades and their varied stone carving to the industrial cylindrical cast-iron heaters. Ely was also luckier with its philanthropists. When a financial crisis in the repair-fund raised the spectre of the cathedral developing the nearby meadows for housing development, John Paul Getty II stepped in and paid the repair bill on the condition that the paddock should remain undeveloped forever.

They say that Ely Cathedral can be seen from the tower of every parish church in the county, and given the flatness of the landscape, I would not doubt it. Some of those parish churches also became familiar landmarks. In a county without the medieval wealth of Suffolk or Norfolk and where low churches with short stumpy towers are the norm, the tall tapering steeples and spires of Willingham, Eltisley, Godmanchester, St Ives, Houghton and Hemingford Abbots stood out as punctuation marks in the countryside. Some were objects of curiosity, such as the bulbous finials on the corners of the battlemented parapets of Cottenham Church or the high pinnacles on the top-heavy tower of Conington near Peterborough, pointed out by my father as a distraction to fractious children in the back seat of the car. So too was the challenge to count as we passed the number of faces of the octagonal and sixteen-sided towers of St Cyriac and St Mary's Churches in Swaffam Priory.

The manager at Price Bailey in Ely would be Nick Pollington who had been a merchant seaman and lorry driver before deciding to make a radical career change and qualify as an accountant.

At the end of the 1980s Price Bailey was able to celebrate this expansion with its 50th anniversary in 1988.

The *Hertfordshire Observer* noted:

There is no great credit in coming 54th in a race (unless it's the London Marathon with its 30,000 runners) but to be ranked 54th in a list of the UK's companies of accountants shows a distinction which, at least, is the envy of numbers 55 and onwards.

The 54th position is occupied by Price Bailey and Partners of Bishop's Stortford, which has double cause for celebration at the moment ... The firm is 50 years old and is moving into bigger, custom-built premises.

Nick Pollington – the new manager at Price Bailey's office in Ely.

It is a real oak-from-acorn story. From its beginning in April 1938 by Leslie Benten, followed shortly after the war by Stanley Price and Reg Bailey, it has now grown to a firm with branches in Cambridge, Harlow, Dunmow, Chingford, Norwich, Newmarket, Saffron Walden and Haverhill.

Senior partner of the whole firm is Vernon Clarke. He recalls coming to the Stortford office shortly after Bailey, as an articled clerk, and admits that that term, which went out of fashion soon afterwards, now has a ring of antiquity.

But it was the beginning of a valuable grounding in the business, so that he can now describe himself as a 'general practitioner' partner. Each of the partners at Bishop's Stortford considers himself a general practitioner, but with specialist skills. For example, Graham Savage (senior partner at Bishop's Stortford office) deals largely with corporate clients; so does Charles Olley, the newest partner at Bishop's Stortford. Michael Nicholls is a specialist with computers, new businesses and farming. Richard Price (son of Stanley) covers all aspects of a practitioner's work.

Taxation, another important aspect of an accountant's work, is looked after by the senior manager, Ian Smith.

The half-century of expansion has been marked not only by the greater numbers and wider expertise of the staff, but also by the burgeoning equipment. Computers along with other technology, all seem to urge the firm forward into the next 50 years … Those computers are not just for the staff's convenience. They fascinate clients and, sooner or later, they ask if their own records can be stored on Price Bailey's disks. The answer is, of course, yes; and by and by, when a client thinks he has enough business to fill a computer of his own, Price Bailey is in a good position to advise on the choice of machine through its associated company, Codap Services.

The Cambridge office also used the opportunity of the 50th anniversary to promote itself. Senior partner, Roger Evans, said:

> We try to offer clients the best of both worlds. By that I mean we are large enough to provide a comprehensive range of financial management services, but small enough to ensure we treat all our clients personally.

The office made it known that specialist services such as the raising of venture capital and advice on Stock Exchange listings for their clients was available now that they had joined the nationwide association of chartered accountants, the UK200 Group. Previously local businesses had been forced to go to expensive City firms for such advice.

On 1 January 1989 E.J.D. Warne, Secretary of The Institute of Chartered Accountants, wrote to Stanley Price, saying:

Dear Mr Price

I write with very great pleasure on behalf of the President and Members of the Council to send you their congratulations and best wishes on your completion of fifty years membership of the Institute.

May I add my own congratulations and wish you many years of continuing membership?

THE 1989 BUSINESS PLAN

Following its considerable expansion in the 1980s the partners put together a comprehensive Business Plan in 1989.

These were the partners of Price Bailey as the Business Plan was published:

VERNON CLARKE FCA	BISHOP'S STORTFORD
GRAHAM HARDY FCA	HARLOW AND CHINGFORD
MICHAEL HORWOOD FCA	NORWICH
GRAHAM SAVAGE FCA	BISHOP'S STORTFORD
ROGER EVANS FCA	CAMBRIDGE, NEWMARKET & ELY
MICHAEL NICHOLLS FCCA	BISHOP'S STORTFORD
RICHARD PRICE FCA	BISHOP'S STORTFORD
ANTHONY SABAN	CAMBRIDGE, NEWMARKET & ELY
PETER BASS FCCA	HARLOW AND CHINGFORD
ANDREW HULME FCA	CAMBRIDGE, NEWMARKET & ELY
LAWRENCE BAILEY FCA	HAVERHILL & SAFFRON WALDEN
PETER GILLMAN FCA	DUNMOW
JOHN RISEBOROUGH FCA	NORWICH
ALASDAIR MACGILLIVRAY ACA	CAMBRIDGE, NEWMARKET & ELY
CHARLES OLLEY ACA	BISHOP'S STORTFORD
PETER CROUCH ACA	TRAINING PARTNER
DAVID ROBINSON ACA	CAMBRIDGE, NEWMARKET & ELY

This was the structure of Price Bailey in 1989:

	Partners	Staff	Turnover year ended 31 May 1989
BISHOP'S STORTFORD Causeway House, 1 Dane Street, Bishop's Stortford, Herts CM23 3BT	5	38	1010
CAMBRIDGE, NEWMARKET AND ELY 93 Regent Street, Cambridge CB2 1AW 167 Green End Road, Chesterton, Cambridge CB4 1RW 7/8 Black Bear Court, High Street, Newmarket, Suffolk CB8 9AF Walsingham Chambers, Butcher's Row, Ely, Cambs CB7 4NA	5	54	1225
DUNMOW The Old Bank House, 5 Stortford Road, Dunmow, Essex CM6 1DA	1	16	235
HARLOW AND CHINGFORD Aylmer House, The High, Harlow, Essex CM20 1DH 59A Station Road, Chingford, London E4 7BJ	2	26	591
HAVERHILL AND SAFFRON WALDEN 1 Queen's Place, Queen Street, Haverhill, Suffolk CB9 9DZ 17 Museum Street, Saffron Walden, Essex CB10 1BN	1	25	455
NORWICH Horse Fair House, 19 St Faiths Lane, Norwich NR1 1NE	2	14	355

In addition the training partner, who is based at Cambridge, serves all offices.

It states as its objectives:

To preserve and enhance the firm's position as a major provincial accounting practice ranking as one of the fifty largest in the United Kingdom.

To preserve the independence of the firm.

To expand the practice within the East Anglian region.

Partners Howard Sears and Peter Bass with Peter Cadle, whose practice in Chingford was bought by Price Bailey.

To achieve this expansion by:

- accepting new clients;
- assisting the growth of existing clients;
- providing additional services to our clients;
- opening new offices where appropriate;
- entering into dominant mergers in new or existing locations;
- acquiring blocks of fees (in special circumstances only).

To continue to serve small, medium and large businesses, individuals and organisations.

To provide a comprehensive range of services of the highest professional and ethical standards to our clients.

To employ competent qualified and experienced professional staff and provide them with progressive and continuing training to enable them to provide the above services.

The plan for the offices was:

They should be prominently situated where possible in areas convenient for clients and professional colleagues.

They should be well maintained so as to present a uniform, clean and modern image.

They should be a pleasant place of work for partners and staff.

Economy of space should be achieved by the use of modern equipment and limiting the space occupied by any individual so far as is practicable.

Premises will usually be leased although the purchase of further properties will be considered in appropriate circumstances.

Staff, of course, were extremely important, and these were to be the aims:

It is the partner's aim that staff progress, be given the appropriate level of responsibility and that their work be interesting and rewarding.

All professional staff will be graded and their careers monitored to assist promotion within the firm.

Reception, secretarial and administrative staff should be offered the same career interests and rewards as professional staff.

Remuneration and benefits should be fixed at market rates with general salary levels (including the effects of inflation) being reviewed on 1 June each year. Inter alia they should take account of:

- ability;
- examination success;
- length of service;
- fee earning capacity.

Students will be encouraged to pursue professional qualifications (appropriate to their level of educational achievement) with one of the following:

- Institute of Chartered Accountants in England and Wales;
- Chartered Association of Certified Accountants;
- Institute of Taxation;
- Association of Accounting Technicians.

Professional and examination training, both internal and external will be provided under supervision and control of the training partner.

Continuing professional education will also be provided under control and supervision of the training partner.

Staff not pursuing a formal professional education will be provided with appropriate training under the control and supervision of the training partner.

Each office should decide its own staffing requirements and keep the staff and training committee notified of these.

All staff should promote the firm and its services to clients, professional contacts and potential clients.

The chargeable time of professional staff will be targeted and monitored as appropriate.

These plans were to be set in motion by an Executive Committee whose composition and frequency of meetings would be:

- The members of the Executive Committee are appointed by the Partnership Committee.

- Members serve for a period of three years.

- The longest serving member shall retire annually and may offer himself for re-election.

- Meetings are to be held as required, with copies of the agenda being circulated to all partners prior to the meetings.

- The minutes of each meeting to be circulated within fourteen days.

And whose terms of reference would be:

- To be responsible for the implementation of partnership policy, and make recommendations to amend the policy as appropriate.

- To ensure that office business plans conform with partnership policy and to meet with the senior partner of each office to review the office's performance in line with the business plan.

- To set target profit figures for each office in line with past performance, general economic position of the office and future expectations after consultation with the local partners in each office.

- To make recommendations as to who should be the senior partner in each office.

- To make recommendations as to the membership of the various partnership committees and set the terms of reference of the committees.

- To receive representations and reports from the other committees and ensure that these committees implement partnership policy.

- To liaise with all offices of the practice and to be available to assist them in management decisions outside the local partners' terms of reference.

- To review the firm's monthly statistics and quarterly accounts, chargeable time and profitability and to generally monitor practice performance.

- To monitor bank positions and authorise requests for overdraft facilities as appropriate.

- To be responsible for the preparation of budgets and half yearly accounts.

- To co-ordinate and review financial and business plans, and make recommendations to the practice in respect of future policy changes.

- To arrange for the audit of client accounts and other procedures at all offices as appropriate.

- To make recommendations to the partnership regarding the partnership agreement, profit sharing ratios and other partnership changes.

- To take decisions and set policy regarding the future funding of the practice.

- To consider and make recommendations on the acquisition of practices or other blocks of fees or approaches to other firms to form an association.

- To consider and make recommendation on approaches made to the practice by other firms.

- To set the criteria that have to be met before an individual can become a partner.

- To receive suggestions and to recommend the appointment of new partners.

These were the Senior Partner representatives:

Graham Savage	Bishop's Stortford
Roger Evans	Cambridge, Newmarket and Ely
Peter Gillman	Dunmow
Graham Hardy	Harlow and Chingford
Lawrence Bailey	Haverhill and Saffron Walden
Michael Horwood	Norwich

A Price Bailey advertisement of 1988.

These were two associations with outside organisations:

Price Bailey Financial Services

This is a joint venture company with insurance brokers Chapman How. Its aim is to provide a comprehensive range of financial services, with appropriate planning, primarily to Price Bailey clients. Michael Horwood and Roger Evans are members of the Price Bailey Financial Services Limited board of directors.

Codap Service Limited

The company is run in conjunction with James Greenall and supplies specialist computer services. Vernon Clarke, Roger Evans and Andrew Hulme are members of the Codap board of directors.

A number of committees were set up:

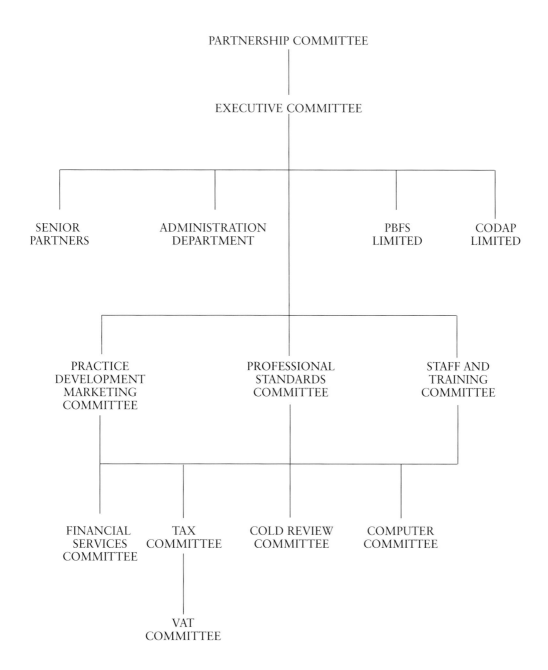

PARTNERSHIP COMMITTEE

EXECUTIVE COMMITTEE

SENIOR
PARTNERS

ADMINISTRATION
DEPARTMENT

PBFS
LIMITED

CODAP
LIMITED

PRACTICE
DEVELOPMENT
MARKETING
COMMITTEE

PROFESSIONAL
STANDARDS
COMMITTEE

STAFF AND
TRAINING
COMMITTEE

FINANCIAL
SERVICES
COMMITTEE

TAX
COMMITTEE

COLD REVIEW
COMMITTEE

COMPUTER
COMMITTEE

VAT
COMMITTEE

7 | Further expansion

RECESSION

By the time of the General Election in April 1992, Britain had suffered a recession which, if not as severe as that of the early 1980s, nevertheless caused a great deal of pain in manufacturing industry and elsewhere in the economy. The Crash of 1987 had been telling the world something, but for a time it was not clear what. Investors were feeling very pleased with themselves by the summer of 1987, and by October the City was wallowing in an orgy of self-love. The Tories were in for another five years (Margaret Thatcher had been comfortably re-elected in June 1987), money – serious money – was there for the taking, the markets were going up after the usual summer hiccup, then BANG! It all stopped. First New York, then Tokyo and Hong Kong, then London, then New York again, then Hong Kong, Tokyo and Sydney, then London, Paris and Frankfurt all turned into screaming, yelling pits of hysteria as the markets lost a year's gain in 24 hours. To exacerbate the situation, the hurricane in Britain three days before prevented many dealers from reaching their screens.

It was only twelve years or 3,000 trading days since the FT 30 index had stood at 147. Now it lost 183.7 in a single day. If anyone thought that was difficult to cope with, the Dow Jones fell by over 500 points, and it was only five years or 1,250 trading days since that index had been around 600. But that of course was part of the reason. The indexes had risen a long way, and once punters wanted to cash in some of their profits there could only be one result. Black Monday, 19 October 1987, was so called after Black Monday in October 1929 – which had itself been named after Black Friday 1869, when a group of punters tried to corner the gold market, causing a panic that led to crash and a depression.

So many records were broken on this Black Monday – biggest one-day fall, biggest volume, more deals on the New York Stock Exchange that day than in the whole of 1950, etc. – that everyone ran out of superlatives, except that no one thought it was particularly superlative. Being the nuclear age, John Phelan, Chairman of the New York Stock Exchange, described it as 'the closest to meltdown I'd ever want to get'. In the same way that almost everyone over the age of 45 can remember exactly what they were doing when they heard that President Kennedy had been shot, every investor will remember what they were doing on 19 October 1987. It was serious. By the middle of Tuesday, as the Dow was plunging again – by then it had lost 800 points in less than five days' trading – the New York Stock Exchange was in touch with the White House and considering the suspension of trading. At that moment the market rallied and, although it might only be a dead cat bounce, it was at least a bounce and it removed the pressure for a moment. If New York had suspended trading, the effect on prices in London would have been catastrophic, as that would have been the only escape hatch. The Hong Kong Exchange did suspend trading, and that exerted extra pressure elsewhere, especially in Sydney. Why were the falls so massive? Prices could not keep going up forever. 'Why not?' asked Sid, who had been persuaded to buy British Gas and other privatised stocks. Good question. No one knew the answer, but they never had before. This did not explain the precipitous plunge. Programme trading by computer and portfolio insurance went a long way to explaining it.

Portfolio insurance had grown dramatically in popularity in the twelve months before the Crash – the pension fund assets in the USA that were managed in this way had grown from $8.5 billion to $60 billion. In simple terms, it meant that by trading in the futures market on the indexes, a portfolio could be insured against a fall. Thus you could buy with impunity, which helped to drive the market up, and if it turned you were covered in the futures market, which would just as certainly drive the market down. In theory this is great, but the concept has, in retrospect, a rather obvious flaw: if the market is falling, not everyone can be a winner or emerge unscathed. Someone has to buy what everyone else wants to sell. In the week before Black Monday, the portfolio insurers had not been able to sell the stock they wanted to, so by the Monday the pressure was immense. On Black Monday itself, as the insurers sold the futures below the prices in the market, no one would buy the actual stocks when the futures showed they could fall much further, and no one wanted the futures while the portfolio insurers were the obvious sellers. The result – a free fall.

There were moments of wry humour. In the US, Alan Greenspan, Chairman of the Federal Reserve Board, was flying to Dallas to make a speech. The markets were falling as he boarded the plane, so he was greatly relieved when he arrived at Dallas to be told that the Dow Jones was down 'Five Oh Eight' – until he realised that the 'Oh' was not a decimal point.

On Tuesday in New York, in spite of another huge fall in London in response to Wall Street's 500-point drop the previous night, we witnessed the classic dead cat bounce, and the Dow gained 200 points in the first hour. Then the insurers moved in again on the futures and down went the market again, 225 points in two hours. There was real panic now – any further falls (and the futures market was signalling another 300 points) would send many dealers to the wall. The futures market in Chicago stopped trading, apparently believing that the decision to close New York had already been taken. As everyone waited, the first sign of a turn came for the little-used Major Market Index in Chicago, where there was a rally. New York 'touched it out'; some corporations helped by announcing that they were buying their own stock; and the day finished with a 100 point gain – the largest ever. The immediate crisis was over. The post-mortem began.

The consumer boom that had built up around the world in the 1980s did not lose its momentum overnight, and most of 1988 was another good year, especially in Britain. Chancellor of the Exchequer Nigel (now Lord) Lawson had read his economic history books and knew that what turned the Wall Street Crash of 1929 into the world Depression of the 1930s was the tightening of credit everywhere and the mistaken attempt to balance budgets. He, and others, were determined that that should not happen this time, and lowered interest rates to maintain liquidity in the financial system.

Unfortunately, he overdid it. Most British consumers are not directly affected by the stock market (though many of them are through their pension funds) and, though the Crash made dramatic headlines and hurt a few large private investors, the mass of people went on spending, confident that their main asset – the house they lived in – was still worth far more than they had paid for it.

The house price spiral was given a final upward twist when Lawson announced the end of double tax relief on mortgages for unmarried couples living together.

However, the new law would not apply until August, and the early summer of 1988 witnessed the final frenzy of house purchase at what, in retrospect, came to be seen as silly prices. What those who were buying failed to notice was that the interest rate cycle had turned. After reducing interest rates at the end of 1987 and the early part of 1988, Lawson realised that the British economy was overheating badly. The mature, some would say sclerotic, British economy could grow only at about 3 per cent before it hit capacity restraints and ran into inflation and balance of payments problems. Lawson took a long time to realise that the economy was growing much faster than this. (One of the Thatcher government's public expenditure economies had been to cut down on the Whitehall department supplying statistics on the economy, and these were taking a long time to become available. It proved to be a very expensive cost saving.) However, by early summer 1988 the overheating was obvious as the inflation rate turned upwards and the balance of payments deficit ballooned alarmingly. Lawson should probably have raised taxes in his 1988 budget instead of reducing them, but the real problem was the amount of liquidity in the economy. He tackled this by raising interest rates.

The only problem was that a national economy is a big ship, and big ships take a long time to stop and turn round. People did not realise the implications – and nor, in all fairness, did most businessmen, financial commentators or politicians. The balance of payments got worse, and interest rates went up again until they eventually reached 15 per cent. This meant that most people were paying 18 – 20 per cent on their overdrafts, loans and mortgages. It may have taken some time to stop the ship, but stop it certainly did, and with some very nasty related and self-feeding consequences.

Not only had house prices risen very sharply in the 1980s, but the financing of them had become very easy – 90, 95 and even 100 per cent loans had become available. On a £100,000 mortgage, 10 per cent was £833 a month – quite a lot of money, but manageable if both partners were earning £1,500 a month. The sums looked differently by the end of 1989, when repayments had moved up to £1,600 a month and one of the jobs looked a little shaky. If the worst happened and one of the partners lost his or her job (and high interest rates also bring recessions), the couple would have to sell the house and move to something cheaper. And it was only then that the real calamity of the house price spiral hit home. The house that had been bought for £110,000 with a £100,000 mortgage could not be sold, certainly not at £110,000, nor at £100,000, nor even at £90,000 or £80,000. It could perhaps be 'given away' at £70,000. The couple faced disaster. They could not keep up the mortgage payments, but if they sold the house they owed the mortgage company £30,000. John Major, who took over from Nigel Lawson as Chancellor when Thatcher determined that he should take the blame for this fiasco, said: 'If it isn't hurting, it isn't working.'

For many it was hurting all right.

At Price Bailey, after all the expansion of the 1980s and the drawing up of the comprehensive Business Plan in 1989, the early 1990s proved to be a very difficult time for the firm.

At least in early 1990, expansion continued when the firm took over the practice of Rodney Wolverson, Griffin and Partners. Wolverson had worked and qualified with Price Bailey in the second half of the 1970s but had left to set up his own firm in Cambridge in 1980. He had specialised in helping smaller businesses and in personal tax.

Rodney Wolverson, whose practice was bought by Price Bailey in 1990.

At the same time, Price Bailey expanded the training function under Peter Crouch by recruiting a new Training Manager, Michael Jerome. Jerome came from a large London practice and brought extensive experience as a consultant and lecturer in the City.

Meanwhile the recession was deepening and Price Bailey did not escape the fallout. Lawrence Bailey remembered that two of the firm's biggest clients were construction companies, Elliot, handled by the Bishop's Stortford office and Emson, handled by the Cambridge office. Price Bailey suffered not only the loss of two clients but bad debts in the form of unpaid fees for previous work.

There were also some management problems within the firm, particularly in

Bishop's Stortford. This was how Graham Hardy, by this time Managing Partner, recalled the situation and how he dealt with it:

The performance of the Bishop's Stortford office had been giving the partners some concern for several years. The chargeable time, recovery rates and profitability were too low and the Executive Committee interviewed each partner at the office in an endeavour to improve matters. After much consultation we made some radical changes to the management of the office.

Finally, on 21 August 1992, Richard Price sent this memo to all the staff at Bishop's Stortford:

I am sure you will all be aware of the sad events of the last 24 hours when three members of our office were made redundant. It is my intention to try to speak to every member of staff within the next few days about the effect of these redundancies on our office and how this affects the remainder of the staff. I enclose a memorandum from Graham Hardy and John Riseborough regarding the situation in the practice and would ask for everyone's co-operation in ensuring that we give an exemplary service to our clients.

To: All Staff
From: Graham Hardy and John Riseborough
21 August 1992

It is with considerable regret that we announce that with effect from today's date, five redundancies will take place at Regent Street, one at Chesterton and three at Bishop's Stortford.

The above redundancies include a senior manager, manager, assistants and administration staff.

The decision, which has been a most difficult and painful one to reach has been made necessary by the effects of the length and severity of the recession. Indeed, we have delayed this action for longer than most of our competitors.

It is our earnest hope that similar action will not be necessary in the future and we would take this opportunity to underline our commitment to our staff and our continuing appreciation of their efforts.

Another sad event of 1991 was the death of Stanley Price at the age of 74. We have seen his achievements in helping to build Price Bailey so that, at the time of his and Reg Bailey's retirement in 1982, the firm had grown to comprise

11 partners and seven offices. His obituary included these details of his life outside Price Bailey:

Away from work Stanley was treasurer and also chairman for 3 years of the East Herts Conservative Association and was a long standing member of Bishop's Stortford Rotary Club, where he was a past president and long time secretary. He was also treasurer during the first 10 years of the Harlow Sports Centre and a keen member of Bishop's Stortford Bowls and Cricket Clubs. He obtained his main relaxation however through playing cards, particularly bridge and solo.

Many of Stanley's friends and acquaintances were aware that his eyesight was not good but few of us knew that he only had the sight of one eye since the age of 7 making his achievements most remarkable. He had many friends and few if any enemies. Price Bailey owes him a lot and will be the poorer without him. He leaves 2 sons Richard (who followed him into Price Bailey) and Andrew and 4 grandchildren.

Richard Price, the very long-serving partner of Price Bailey, who eventually became its popular Chairman.

SPECIALIST SERVICES

In spite of the recession of the early 1990s and the problems it brought for Price Bailey, the firm was still determined to pursue the expansion of its specialist services. Richard Price said:

> Over the last few years, we have put considerable effort and resources into setting up these specialist units. There is no doubt that this was the right thing to do, as we are now well placed to provide a considerably more rounded service to our developing clients.

One of the specialist units, based in the Bishop's Stortford office, was the Corporate Finance Department. It was managed by Paul Storer, who said:

> In spite of this deep recession, there are still a surprising number of good businesses seeking to expand and which need fresh capital, good management or acquisition opportunities.
>
> We have taken many enquiries from businesses such as these and have been successful in introducing individuals or businesses able to offer capital or expertise, merger or acquisition opportunities.

Another specialist unit set up in the early 1990s was the Small Business Unit led by Andrew Hulme. This unit was aimed at helping businesses with a turnover of less than £50,000 to grow. (As it happens, the author's publishing business, Icon Books Ltd, was founded in 1992 and Price Bailey has certainly helped it grow. It has not been dramatic growth but, in 2013, 20 years later, the turnover will be over £2.5 million on which a healthy profit will be made.)

One of the difficulties most small businesses had was dealing with the various tax authorities and Ian Smith, a tax specialist, was a key member of the Personal Tax unit. He spent a lot of time in the late 1980s and early 1990s advising Lloyds underwriters, whose tax problems were adding to the severe difficulties Lloyds was suffering at the time.

Continuing on this theme, the *Herts & Essex Observer* wrote in 1993 under a photograph of Richard Price, Paul Martin, Howard Sears and Alison Hughes, and the heading:

(opposite page)
Causeway House, Price Bailey's office in Bishop's Stortford to the present day.

PRICE BAILEY – much more than accountants

It has often been said that the difference between a thriving and a struggling business is access to good accountancy services.

The true professionals can make all the difference, both to companies and individuals, and in the most successful relationships the accountant is more than a business adviser, also a friend and ally, confidant and confessor.

With legislation ever more complex and following the ravages of the recession, there has never been such a call for the best accountancy advice, and, in the Bishop's Stortford area, we are fortunate in having one of the longest-established and leading regional, multi-office practices in the centre of the business community.

We refer to PRICE BAILEY, Chartered Accountant and Independent Financial Advisers, of Causeway House, 1 Dane Street, and established in the town for over 50 years.

No-one can accuse PRICE BAILEY of not moving with the times: in addition to the conventional accountancy services, they offer a wide variety of specialist help within their specifically tailored units. After all, with the right advice and guidance, the small, start-up business of today is the potential high-flying company of tomorrow.

PRICE BAILEY do not concentrate on size, but on service – no client is too small or too large, be they sole trader, partnership or company. Whatever the size of the business, or its aspirations for growth, PRICE BAILEY have the experience and knowledge to complement the business. The firm believes all businesses benefit from year-round professional advice – suggesting, warning, interpreting and, where possible, relieving clients of financial chores.

Bishop's Stortford is a member of PRICE BAILEY'S Southern Group, which also consist of offices in Chingford, Dunmow and Harlow. The resident partners of the Group are Peter Bass, Peter Gillman, Graham Hardy, Michael Nicholls, Charles Olley and Richard Price.

All partners and managers follow the PRICE BAILEY ethos of taking close personal involvement with individual clients' affairs; a partnership both professional and personal. They are very proud that the majority of their new clients are introduced on the recommendation of individuals and businesses that are already advised by PRICE BAILEY.

One of the firm's original departments based in Bishop's Stortford is the Personal Tax Unit, led by Ian Smith, which matches the expertise of many of the City's leading firms. Clients' requirements range from the solving of individual, one-off tax problems, through helping with annual tax returns, to complex tax and investment panning exercises.

With their diverse skills, staff of the highest calibre and use of the latest technology, PRICE BAILEY offers a comprehensive service covering every aspect of business and finance for all types of client small or large, professional or commercial.

Richard Price commented 'The whole firm is looking forward to the next few years, taking on the challenges of substantial changes in economic activity, tax legislation and technology. PRICE BAILEY is in a unique position to help clients take advantage of all such opportunities.

PRICE BAILEY
CHARTERED ACCOUNTANTS AND INDEPENDENT FINANCIAL ADVISERS

SERVICES AVAILABLE

Audit and accounting
* audit of accounts
* preparation of annual accounts
* preparation of management
  accounts
* forecast and reports for banks
  and management use
* setting up and maintenance
  of trust

Taxation services
* VAT returns and VAT planning
* tax returns
* personal tax and financial planning
* preparation of business tax computations
* inheritance tax advice
* corporate tax planning
* payroll bureau

Corporate finance
* advice on setting up in business
* preparation of business plans
* help in securing finance
* USM and over-the-counter flotations
* business acquisitions and disposals
* share valuations

Investment matters
* acquisition of capital and government grants
* investment advice
* pensions
* insurances

Corporate law
* company secretarial duties
* company law advice
* company formations

Systems
* advice on book-keeping systems
* advice on computer installations
* in-house company facilities

AND MANY MORE ...

In 1993 Graham Hardy retired as Managing Partner and became Chairman. John Riseborough took over as Managing Partner and, in July 1994, a new Strategic Plan was put in place. It ran to no fewer than 35 pages and laid out a Mission Statement followed by 10 Practice Objectives.

The Mission Statement was: 'To be an outstanding regional practice of chartered accountants.'

The Practice Objectives were:

1) To retain the status of a firm of practising chartered accountants.

2) To provide a quality service to our clients.

3) To provide a range of services.

4) To recruit, develop and retain quality people.

5) To have a quality client base.

6) To remain an independent practice.

7) To achieve and maintain an acceptable level of practice profitability.

8) To maintain the base of the practice in East Anglia.

9) To operate from premises of a suitable standard.

10) To achieve quality management of the practice.

It was to be hoped that this plan would be easier to implement than the one of 1989 which had suffered from events largely out of the firm's control.

Certainly there was some rationalisation of offices as the Chesterton office was closed in October 1995, with the staff moving to Cambridge, Haverhill in January 1996 with the staff moving to Newmarket, and Dunmow in February 1996 with the staff moving to Bishop's Stortford.

Nevertheless, Price Bailey continued to grow and prosper in the millennium. In March 2001 they moved offices in Harlow and Richard Price sent this e-mail to 'All Price Bailey Personnel':

From tomorrow and over the weekend, the Harlow team are leaving Aylmer House, where we have been for the last forty years and moving in to our own self-contained building. Our new address is Park House, 1 Sarbir Industrial Park, Cambridge Road, Harlow, with the same telephone and fax numbers. The lines are being switched tomorrow and there may be a short interruption in service. We are in BT's hands.

The new offices have their own parking and are a bright and pleasant environment, compared to the very old and tired building we are leaving.

It is interesting that the first mention of the Harlow office in the archives was in April 1947, when the address mentioned was Gothic House in the old High Street, long before the New Town was built. As soon as Harlow New Town started to be built, the office moved into premises in The Stow, the first shop/office area. We moved to the High in 1961 into lavish new premises, which had central heating!! How times have changed!

I am sure everyone wishes the Harlow team well.

BISHOP'S STORTFORD EXPANDS

In spite of the general economic difficulties of the first half of the 1990s, Price Bailey's Bishop's Stortford office continued to prosper and in1996 it moved into the whole of Causeway House in Dane Street. The firm had occupied two floors since 1988. It took the opportunity to merge the Dunmow office into Bishop's Stortford. By this time Price Bailey had a total of fourteen partners in its various offices and employed 150 people. Fifty of the employees were in the new enlarged Bishop's Stortford office, of whom four were partners. The first was Peter Gillman who had been at the Dunmow office for 20 years and was now the managing partner of the Southern Group which included Bishop's Stortford, Harlow and Chingford. The others were Richard Price, Mike Nicholls and Charles Olley.

Stansted in pre-First World War days.

In an advertisement in the *Herts & Essex Observer,* Price Bailey noted that:

To complement the traditional accountancy services offered, Price Bailey has a number of specialist departments, including those in such areas as:

VAT
Corporate Finance
Personal and Corporate Tax
Book-keeping and Payroll

Membership of the UK200 Group of Practising Accountants, an association of independent firms, also provides access to a nationwide network of other accountancy firms and international connections.

Peter Gillman did not want to lose the personal touch as Price Bailey grew bigger and used humour in selling the firm's services, epitomised by this letter:

9 May 1996

Mr A Roe
ADRO Technologies Limited
8 Raynham Road
BISHOP'S STORTFORD
Herts

Dear Mr Roe,

HOW MANY CHARTERED ACCOUNTANTS DOES IT TAKE TO CHANGE A LIGHT BULB?

As a Chartered Accountant, I have to accept that my profession does attract this kind of joke. It is an occupational hazard!

By no means do all Chartered Accountants deserve the reputation of being as exciting as drying paint or Stephen Hendry winning the World Snooker title.

As the Group Managing Partner of Price Bailey, I do try to develop a more human approach to our client's needs; it is all too easy to report on financial information without relating to the people and the business that is responsible for those results.

Of course our clients want their periodic or year-end figures produced quickly and cost effectively, but most also want a view on what accounts for those results and what might be done to improve or maintain them. I hope that is where the independent views of your accountant can really help.

You may have seen in the local press that Price Bailey has recently expanded their operation in Bishop's Stortford and I have now moved my base to our refurbished offices. I am now meeting with local businesses to tell them a little more about our style of approach and the services that we can offer from Causeway House and would really welcome the chance to come and have a chat. It will not cost you anything and I can tell you how we might help you.

I can also tell you how many Chartered Accountants it takes to change a light bulb!

Yours sincerely

Peter Gillman
PRICE BAILEY

P.S. Nothing against Stephen Hendry; he is a superb snooker player!

'PRICE BAILEY WERE FABULOUS'

One recipient of this letter from Gillman was Barry van Danzig. He was amused by it and invited Gillman to his office. His company, Wastepack Ltd, became a new, interesting and valued client.

It was founded in 1994 as Wastelink, by Barry van Danzig who had been brought up in the East End of London and left school at the age of 14 without a single O level (he later passed in English after studying at night school). He worked first in a factory then a shoe shop. He became a salesman and sold for various roof light companies before joining a skylight manufacturer called William Cox, who made canopies for Spitfire fighter aircraft during the Second World War. He organised a management buy-out but unfortunately inherited a debtor who failed to pay and van Danzig's company was forced into liquidation.

He secured a job with Biffa, the waste disposal company, and it was there he conceived the idea that would make him a fortune. He noticed that businesses, including supermarkets and other retailing chains with branches all over the country, were organising their waste disposal on an outlet by outlet basis. He thought, 'Why don't I go to the head offices and offer to take care of all their waste disposal? They would then have only one supplier and one invoice for their waste disposal instead of hundreds of both'.

It worked and sales grew to no less than £30 million within just three years.

Unfortunately van Danzig then hit another problem. His partner absconded with most of the cash they had earned. At this point, in 1998, he thought he had better organise a well-respected accountancy firm to take care of his finances. He looked in Yellow Pages and, coincidentally, as we saw above, received one of Peter Gillman's amusing letters. He rang Gillman, they got on well, and Price Bailey were hired. Van Danzig said later:

> Price Bailey were fabulous. They put in Lynne Cullis as the auditor, I recruited her as our Finance Director and she is now our Chief Executive.

Two years later Wastepack (as it was called by this time) was approached by a venture capital group and van Danzig sold half the company and retired with £6.5 million. The venture capital company was Duke Street Capital and Price Bailey organised the sale. Unfortunately, the new management did not run the company well and began to lose money. They also brought in Price Waterhouse Cooper (PWC) as auditor instead of Price Bailey.

Van Danzig was still a minority shareholder and in 2005 he bought back into the company and re-appointed Price Bailey as auditor.

STANSTED AIRPORT

The Price Bailey Bishop's Stortford office has benefited greatly from the expansion of Stansted Airport since the 1980s.

The airfield opened in 1943 during the Second World War when it was used by both the Royal Air Force and the United States Army Air Force as a base for bomber aircraft and as a major maintenance depot. At the end of the war the Americans withdrew and the airfield was taken over by the Air Ministry and it was then used by a Maintenance Unit of the RAF for storage purposes. It was also used between March 1946 and August 1947 for housing German prisoners of war awaiting repatriation. In 1949 the Ministry of Civil Aviation took control and the airport began to be used by a member of UK charter airlines. However, in 1954, the US military returned and extended the runway in anticipation of a transfer to the North Atlantic Treaty Organisation (NATO). However, this transfer never occurred and the airport continued to be used by civil airlines. Also, during the 1960s, 1970s and early 1980s, the Fire Service Training School, controlled by the Ministry of Transport and Civil Aviation, now the Civilian Aviation Authority, was based on the eastern side of the airfield.

In 1966 Stansted was placed under the control of the British Airports Authority (BAA) and airlines, mainly holiday charter ones, used it to escape the higher charges of Heathrow and Gatwick. Both the government and BAA had plans to develop Stansted to relieve the growing congestion at Heathrow and Gatwick.

Stansted's first terminal building opened in 1969 but the big expansion came in the late 1980s after the government approved in 1984 a plan to develop Stansted in two phases which would give the airport an annual capacity of 15 million passengers. Building began in 1988 and was completed in 1991.

The terminal building was designed by the renowned Foster Associates and features a 'floating' roof, supported by a space frame of inverted-pyramid roof trusses, creating the impression of a stylised swan in flight. The layout of the terminal was designed so that an unobstructed flow of passengers could move from arrival at the short-stay car park, on through the check-in hall, then through security and on to the departure gates all on the same level.

The expansion and growth of passengers was certainly achieved, particularly on the back of the boom in low-cost air travel. In the 12 months to October 2007 no fewer than 24 million passengers passed through the airport. Thanks to Ryanair choosing it as its main base in south-east England (Easyjet chose Luton) Dublin airport became the leading destination.

Needless to say, all this expansion needed to be serviced by a growing number of companies based either in the terminal building itself or near the airport. Price Bailey was not slow to capitalise in offering its services to these expanding or brand-new businesses.

One very successful operator at Stansted has been Titan Airways, currently a client of Price Bailey. It was founded in February 1988, was subject to a management buy-out in February 1992 and is currently owned by Gene Wilson and the venture capital form, 3i.

Titan works on behalf of cruise ship companies such as Fred Olsen Cruises, Princess Cruises and Cunard and it operates charter flights for British tour companies. It flies from Birmingham, Bristol, Manchester, Gatwick and Stansted to French and Swiss ski destinations. Furthermore, in 2011 it announced that it secured a twelve-month contract from the UK Ministry of Defence to provide a twice-weekly air service to the Falkland Isles.

The world and the UK economy recovered in the second half of the 1990s and Price Bailey prospered too. By 1999 the firm had grown to become the 42nd largest accountant by fee income in the country. Its income was £5.8 million, it

Stansted Airport brought growth to the area.

had 20 partners with a fee income per partner of £290,000 and it employed 91 professional staff.

By 2000 Price Bailey was growing steadily again and *Accountancy Age* noted in July 2000: 'Price Bailey expanded its management consultancy by 700% to £800,000.'

And the firm continued to grow. In spite of the fall-out from the collapse of the dot-com bubble, *Accountancy Age* was able to report in June 2002:

> It was the mid-tier that saw exceptional rises. Armstrong Watson at number 28, notched up a percentage rise of 21.9% while Price Bailey, in the number 38 slot, topped that with a rise of 32%.

(opposite page) Stansted Airport grew ever larger.

Helping the growth was Price Bailey's determination to keep pace with the rapidly growing computerisation of business activity, not least in the accountancy area. Alan Becker, the Sage manager at Price Bailey was able to say:

> We are pleased to join forces with Sage to provide an enhanced service to our clients. This agreement will help us achieve our aim to be the first choice provider for business advisory services for small to medium-sized businesses across the country.

At the time, Price Bailey was one of the first Sage accredited Solution Centres and the only Chartered Accountancy and Business Advisory firm in the Cambridge region to have been accredited by Sage (UK) Ltd.

8 | Uncertain times

A MARVELLOUS JOB
9/11
LLP
'PREDICTION IS VERY DIFFICULT'
MEASUREMENT PROJECT

A MARVELLOUS JOB

In June 2001, Peter Gillman succeeded John Riseborough as managing partner of Price Bailey. Gillman had joined Price Bailey from school in 1970 and worked initially in the Harlow office. He qualified as a chartered accountant in 1974. He moved to the Great Dunmow office and then to Bishop's Stortford. He moved back to the Great Dunmow office in 1977 where he became a partner and managed that office until it was closed in February 1996 when he returned to Bishop's Stortford.

Gillman said:

> John Riseborough has done a marvellous job, leading the firm through a period of enormous change to our current position as one of the UK's top 50 chartered accountancy practices. I now hope to build on that success by keeping us one step ahead in what continues to be a fast evolving market place.

He said that service innovation, coupled with the firm's commitment to staff training and development, will continue to be the critical success factors of the future, adding:

> The accountancy business has probably seen more change over the past five years than it did in the previous hundred. We were one of the first regional firms to recognise the need to broaden our services away from traditional regulatory work into the more dramatic arena of business consultancy and this has proved an outstanding success with our clients.

Gillman immediately faced an unexpected problem, as did the rest of the world.

9/11

On 11 September 2001, which became known as 9/11 (the telephone number used for emergencies in the USA, a coincidence certainly appreciated by the perpetrators of the attack) the world was stunned when at just before 9.00am Eastern Standard Time a passenger airliner was flown into one of the Twin Towers in downtown Manhattan, New York. A few may have thought it was an accident but when, forty minutes later, another airliner was flown into the second tower, no one was under the illusion that these were anything but deliberate attacks. This realisation was reinforced when another aircraft was flown into the Pentagon in Washington, and finally when a fourth aircraft crashed in Pennsylvania, killing all those on board.

Two and a half hours that changed the history of the world:

7:59 AM	Mohamed Atta boards American Airlines Flight 11, which under his control will crash into the World Trade Center
8:18 AM	American Airlines Flight 11 is taken over by Mohamed Atta and other hijackers
8:46 AM	American Airlines Flight 11 crashes into the World trade Center North Tower
9:03 AM	United Airlines Flight 175 crashes into the World Trade Center South Tower
9:37 AM	American Airlines Flight 77 crashes into the Pentagon
9:59 AM	South Tower of World Trade Center collapses
10:03 AM	United Airlines Flight 93 crashes into a farm in Shanksville, Pennsylvania
10:28 AM	North Tower of World Trade Center collapses

The mighty USA was under attack on its home soil, the first time since the Japanese attack on Pearl Harbor in December 1941. The President, George W. Bush, was visiting a school in Florida, and was quickly bundled into the presidential aircraft and flown around until it could be ascertained how serious the situation was and whether any more attacks were likely. Needless to say, all other aircraft throughout the USA were grounded.

In the very short term, the effects for business were little short of calamitous. Everyone seemed to freeze. The truth was that there was a mild recession in place anyway. The so-called dot-com bubble had burst the year before, after any company involved with the internet had seen its shares rise to ridiculous and, with hindsight, clearly unsustainable, heights.

Price Bailey did not allow the 9/11 disaster to divert them and in April 2002 bought the practice Stephenson Davies, a four-partner firm of accountants with offices in Ely, March and Newmarket. The firm had been founded 60 years earlier. This merger followed the success of a strategic alliance and joint venture in Newmarket. In the press release issued, Andrew Youles, the Stephenson Davies resident March partner said:

> Although Stephenson Davies has always been able to offer excellent core services such as audit, accountancy and tax compliance, it is more difficult to provide the additional services that our clients have come to expect.
>
> These include corporate finance, financial services, personal and corporate tax consultancy, detailed VAT planning, recruitment, people management, business development and profit improvement work.
>
> This merger will enable these and other specialist services to be provided to our existing and future clients.

Nick Pollington the Price Bailey resident Ely partner added:

> This is an exciting development for the firm. It provides tremendous scope for future expansion in March, and reflects our strategy of consolidating in those areas where we have existing offices – in this case Ely and Newmarket.
>
> We believe that there is a growing marketplace for local firms, serving the local community, that are able to provide a full range of services to their clients – delivered with honesty and integrity.
>
> I'm particularly looking forward to helping Andrew in March, which I see as an important growth area.

Trevor Smith, a farmer's son, had joined Stephenson Davies in 1977 and, after a full-time foundation course in Norwich, four years as an articled clerk and one year at accountants Spicer and Pegler in Cambridge, qualified as a chartered accountant in 1983. He became a partner in 1989 and managing partner in 1999.

When the two firms, both members of the UK200 Group, merged in 2002, Smith became the managing partner of the Ely office. Since then he has spent much of his time on corporate finance and his largest client with a turnover of over £200 million is the Turners haulage business based near Newmarket.

Aside from the 9/11 disaster, the view of Peter Gillman and the Board in 2004 was that Price Bailey had too many partners – there were 27 – and too many offices and was being held back by disjointed and inconsistent services. Turnover of the firm was £7 million and profitability was poor.

LLP

In early 2004, Price Bailey became a Limited Liability Partnership (LLP). Peter Gillman said:

> While retaining the style of practice inherent in partnership, we feel the time now right to add a sensible measure of protection for our partners in an increasingly litigious market. The change means that partners are no longer jointly and severally liable for all the firm's debts – a position that has recently led to the worldwide destruction of a major international accounting firm, Arthur Andersen.

In the United Kingdom LLPs are governed by the Limited Liability Partnership Act 2000 (in Great Britain). A UK Limited Liability Partnership is a corporate body – that is to say, it has a continuing legal existence independent of its members, as compared to a Partnership which may (in England and Wales it would not) have a legal existence dependent upon its membership.

A UK LLP's members have a collective ('joint') responsibility, to the extent that they may agree in an 'LLP agreement', but no individual ('several') responsibility for each other's actions. As with a limited company or a corporation, members in an LLP cannot, in the absence of fraud or wrongful trading, lose more than they invest.

The LLP structure is commonly used by accountants, as a company may not act as auditor to another company. LLPs are also becoming more common among firms in the legal profession such as solicitors and patent attorneys that by law are prohibited from incorporating as companies.

'PREDICTION IS VERY DIFFICULT'

The two years 2003 and 2004 were not good ones for Price Bailey, which was frustrating, especially to Peter Gillman, and it was decided in June 2004 that Price Bailey should be run as a business with an elected Board of Management. The first Board, all elected with a large mandate, were:

Peter Gillman, who was elected Managing Director
Charles Olley
Colin Long
Martin Clapson
Nick Mayhew

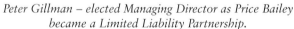

Peter Gillman – elected Managing Director as Price Bailey became a Limited Liability Partnership.

Charles Olley – elected a Director of the Board of Management.

The Board's first meeting took place in October 2004. It was decided that there should be a consolidation into five offices: Norwich, Ely, Cambridge, Bishop's Stortford and North London. Other offices should be closed and six partners would either be retired or leave the firm with agreed packages.

More, and more profitable, clients were needed and Price Bailey's core values would need to be stressed. These were consistency, best practice, continuous improvement and value to all. Furthermore, every contract would need to tick three boxes. It must be right for the client, right for the relevant partner and right for the team handling the contract. The important aim was to try and understand the whole of the client by asking a whole range of questions.

In 2005 Peter Gillman produced a 'Practice Update'. It began with a quotation from the famous Niels Bohr: 'Prediction is very difficult, especially if it is about the future.'

He noted that in 2004 Price Bailey's turnover had been £10 million and profit

£300,000 which were both considerably better than 2001. There were eight offices and 26 partners. In the Board's view, the smaller offices should be closed over a period of time and the retirement of six of the 26 partners organised by March 2005.

New governance would be instituted whereby a Managing Director would be elected every three years and he would be supported by a small elected board. Regional management would be abandoned and replaced with departmentalisation. In 2006 it was decided that from 1 April 2007 the whole firm would be run as a meritocracy with profit sharing.

The reporting to the partners from the regional set-up of the Southern Group consisting of Bishop's Stortford, Harlow, Chingford and North London, the Cambridge Group – Cambridge, Newmarket, Saffron Walden and Ely – and Norwich, was changed to reporting to a board consisting of just four people. The regional structure was abandoned in favour of a profit-sharing group with group pricing of all services. Cross-practice departments covering client services were set up.

Those services were organised in 2007:

- Private Client, which included Financial Planning
- Corporate
- Small Business (now called Business Services)

By 2005 Price Bailey had moved up to 36th place in the top 50 accountancy firms. Lawrence Bailey told *Business Weekly*:

> From five locations in Cambridge, Bishop's Stortford, Ely, Norwich and North London we enjoy great relationships with hundreds of large regional and entrepreneurial businesses, many thousands of small businesses and private clients.

MEASUREMENT PROJECT
(initiated by Martin Clapson)

In spite of good progress there were concerns as to whether the firm was using its time to the greatest effect, and a Measurement Project was organised to ask these questions: What behaviours do we want to encourage?

The answer was – we want to encourage all our team members to spend as much time as possible with:

Clients
Other team members discussing client issues
Potential clients

Colin Long – also elected a Director of the Board of Management.

Spending more time with clients will achieve:

>Client feeling valued
Increase cross selling opportunities
Gain extra revenue from that client
Reduce risk of client leaving PB

Spending more time with potential clients will achieve:

>More opportunities to win more work
Win more work
Fees and profits will increase

It had been noticed that some of the team did the above and some did not, who seemed to be worried that if they spent more time with clients or discussing client issues with other team members they would show:

Poor recovery rates
Poor chargeable hours

And that if they spent more time with potential clients they would also show:

Poor chargeable hours

Martin Clapson – also elected a Director of the Board of Management.

Therefore, it was proposed to:

1. Replace the terminology of *chargeable time* with *client time*
   Include a new service code called CONTACT
   Code would have zero cost
   Must complete comment box
   Total time spent with client and/or discussing client issues would be measured positively
   Recovery rates would not be affected as the 'contact' time would have nil value
   This would remove the old discouragement
   Total client time would be measured

2. Set up a client code TARGET
   Time meeting/working on specific potential 'target' would be charged to TARGET client code
   TARGET time would be included with an individual's total client time
   Old discouragement gone
   Total time with clients and specific potentials would be positively measured and encouraged

The conclusion was:

   If we get it right, we really do encourage the right behaviour, i.e.:
   – more time with clients
   – more time discussing client issues
   – more time with potentials

Consequently our business will change dramatically.

By 2008 the business world was becoming tougher. In the UK, there had been a number of unhelpful events including:

• The rescue of Northern Rock whose troubles had been brought about by borrowing short and lending long.
• The raising of the capital gains tax rate from 10 to 18 per cent, a rise of no less than 80 per cent, on the sale of business assets.
• New loans in the USA, bundled into complex financial instruments and sold to bankers all over the world who were looking to save tax on their bonuses.

- A huge increase in the previous year of the price of oil which had doubled in just 12 months.

The accountancy profession was not unaffected and Gillman pointed to the problems at RSM Rhodes which had to be rescued by Grant Thornton, as well as to others.

Price Bailey was determined it was going to weather any recession and emerge stronger than ever. While general economic conditions at home were challenging, fortunately the firm was operating in a prosperous area. As *Accountancy Age* put it in August 2008:

> The county (Hertfordshire) has a lot going for it: a good rail system, accessibility to London, the Midlands and the North; excellent private and state schools, stunning countryside and proximity to international airports.
>
> It has also become well-known for housing many corporate headquarters, including DSG, Tesco, Ocado, J.D. Wetherspoon, Comet and BAE Systems.

Nick Mayhew – also elected a Director of the Board of Management.

Nevertheless, the general business scene was challenging with a number of companies, especially in property and construction, struggling. At Price Bailey, Charles Olley said:

> Business around East Anglia is not too bad. Our clients are weathering the storms fairly robustly, although recovery is taking time. We are seeing more demand for outsourcing payroll and the whole accounts function. There are price pressures and people are taking longer to pay. Like others we are looking aggressively for new business but big firms are pretty defensive. They don't like losing business any more than we do.

Growth, at 14 per cent, was good but well down on the previous year's 38 per cent. Fee income for Price Bailey in 2009 was £14.7 million putting them at 37th in the Top 50.

9 | We must be in London

A City office
Why the City?
Collapse in Confidence

A CITY OFFICE

In 2005 Price Bailey began to consider the opening of an office in the City of London. This would be a bold move as the firm had always considered itself to be an East Anglian operation. You will remember that from the 1950s through to the 1990s expansion had centred around the A11. The firm did have an office in Highams Park in north London but the City would be a different prospect altogether. Clearly a feasibility study would need to be carried out and Peter Gillman and Howard Sears masterminded it.

The Business Reasons for the move fell under four headings:

Business Development

There would be new market opportunities for compliance. It would provide a larger market for consulting services. Furthermore, there would be greater credibility for those consulting services. On the horizon were the Olympics to be held in London in 2012.

London was awarded the 2012 Olympics in July 2005. Peter Gillman saw this as a great opportunity and rang Howard Sears to suggest they look at the possibility of opening a London office. Gillman had already spent 18 months networking in London and the Olympics award acted as a catalyst to go for an office in the City. He had noted that when the Olympics were staged in Barcelona the passengers travelling through the airport had jumped from about two million to 21 million and, more significantly, had continued to rise (by 2012 it had increased to 34 million).

Raise Price Bailey Brand Awareness

The move would build a stronger Price Bailey profile across the whole East Anglian Region. It would change the identity from that of just a regional firm.

Recruitment and Retention

The catchment area for recruiting good candidates would be widened. Those candidates would receive a more attractive offering. It would also bring better prospects for existing partners and employees and open up new lifestyle opportunities.

Profitability

The City office would operate in an area in a higher employment environment and there should be greater volumes of added value work. The prospects for more rapid growth would be enhanced.

London itself was, at 7.2 million people (expected to grow to 8 million by 2016), the largest city in Europe, and was recognised as the leading business centre in Europe. It also acted as a bridge between Europe and the USA. In terms of size London dwarfed all the other large cities in the UK. Birmingham had a population of 970,000, Glasgow 630,000, Liverpool 469,000, Leeds 443,000, Sheffield 439,000, Edinburgh 430,000, Bristol 421,000, Manchester 394,000 and Leicester 331,000. Furthermore, on top of the 7.2 million London residents, over one million people entered London between 7 and 10am every working day. The cities that already housed Price Bailey offices had populations of 174,000 (Norwich), 115,000 (Bishop's Stortford), 113,000 (Cambridge) and 84,000 (Ely).

In London there were over 13,000 overseas owned companies, with 1.3 million people employed in financial services and the professions. 25 per cent of the world's largest financial companies had their European headquarters in London. There were 250,000 VAT registered businesses in London of which 155,000 were in Inner London, 38,500 in Westminster and 12,500 in the City. Again, to put this into the existing Price Bailey context, Bishop's Stortford and Harlow had 5,800 VAT registered businesses, Highams Park 4,900, Cambridge 3,600, Norwich 3,400 and Ely 3,200.

The number of solicitors in each area also emphasised the potential of the

City where there were 294 firms of solicitors in contrast to Cambridge 38, Bishop's Stortford and Harlow 17, Norwich 12, Highams Park 15 and Ely 7.

Nor was the City a difficult place to get to from other Price Bailey offices. Journey times by train were Norwich 1 hour 55 minutes, Ely I hour 35 minutes, Cambridge 1 hour 10 minutes, Bishop's Stortford 37 minutes and Highams Park 23 minutes.

WHY THE CITY?

In short, why should Price Bailey open an office in the City?

> It was a centre of excellence for its target market.
> It was a networking centre for the whole of London.
> It enjoyed good transport links to the rest of London.
> It also had good transport links to the rest of the Price Bailey offices.
> It provided a credible profile for Price Bailey clients.
> It provided a credible profile for Price Bailey recruitment.
> It provided an extra facility for other Price Bailey offices.

The target market offerings would be those who needed professional accounting services, consultancy and corporate advice and the market would include networking, approaches to the London Chamber of Commerce and the Institute of Directors as well as presentations and seminars to other professional bodies.

As part of its new strategy Price Bailey was already focussing on sectors. Now, using its own experience of change management gained from coping with new legislation and regulations – such as the introduction of Limited Liability Partnerships – the partners marketed services to professional services firms such as lawyers, surveyors, property consultants and other accountants. Sears said:

> A lot of information that we're using to assist other professional services firms is a result of having tested it on ourselves.

In November 2006 it was agreed that the London office should be leased and in the middle of 2007 an office with just four people was opened in Eldon Street. At the end of 2007 Price Bailey bought Coombes Wales Quinnell in Baker Street. Two partners of the latter, Ian Coombes and Richard Vass, with a team of seven, including manager, Ben Mari, moved from Baker Street into the Eldon Street office. (Unfortunately, Ian Coombes tragically died in October 2009.)

(above) The City – Price Bailey felt they needed to have an office there. (Works in Print/Richard Osbourne)

*(below) Howard Sears, Charles Olley, Ian Coombes, Peter Gillman and Richard Vass
celebrating the Coombes Wales Quinnell merger with Price Bailey.*

Peter Gillman said:

Earlier this year we opened an office in the City of London and we were keen to build on our credentials as a genuine London practice. We are an ambitious firm that have been around for nearly 70 years and CWQ are a like-minded firm with an established reputation. This merger will open up new markets including the entertainment industry and create specialist client sectors.

The end of the Eldon Street office lease and continued growth prompted a move to Old Broad Street, adjacent to Liverpool Street and therefore Liverpool Street Station and this office now employs 50 people.

Richard Vass, a partner at Coombes Wales Quinnell and now a partner at Price Bailey.

By 2010, it was working with about 40 law firms on a regular basis and off the back of that work was winning plenty of referrals.

Once Price Bailey had expanded into Guernsey (see below), the City office was able to work closely with the Guernsey office in respect of international opportunities.

Perhaps uniquely, the firm had developed new products as well as branching out into new service lines. PPR, or Partner Performance Review, which was a confidential 360-degree appraisal process, was just one of the products with which the firm had enjoyed success. Again, this was based on work that Price Bailey originally developed for internal purposes and went on to sell to its clients, allowing the firm to move into value-added services.

LPP conversion was another product that included a conversion pack so that professional service firms would avoid doing the research themselves. Another product was outsourced management accounting – essential for businesses looking for bank borrowing – which the firm was marketing not just to the legal sector but to others too.

COLLAPSE IN CONFIDENCE

The first signs of trouble appeared in 2007 when the former building society turned bank, Northern Rock, based in the North-East of England, suffered rumours that it may have overlent and was in danger of becoming insolvent. These rumours led to panic amongst some customers and queues formed outside many Northern Rock branches full of people wanting to withdraw their money. The Bank of England was forced to rescue the situation.

Calm returned but this Northern Rock fiasco proved to be a portent of much worse to come. In September 2008 the American investment bank, Lehman Brothers, suffered the same problems as Northern Rock and this time there was no rescue. This led to a worldwide collapse in confidence and a worldwide recession. In the UK, other banks which had made unwise loans were also in serious trouble. Foremost was the Royal Bank of Scotland. They were followed by Lloyds TSB who had been persuaded by Victor Blank and Gordon Brown to buy HBOS, the merged Halifax Building Society and Bank of Scotland.

As it happened, 2008 was the year of Price Bailey's seventieth birthday and the firm held a party at Chilford Barn near Cambridge to celebrate. The evening coincided with financial dramas in the USA. Earlier in the week, the US

Government had been forced to take over two of the country's largest mortgage companies, Freddie Mac and Fannie Mae, and in Europe governments were talking of a major recession and a possible Eurozone crisis.

Managing Director, Peter Gillman, made a speech to the assembled guests in which he spoke of the achievement of the firm lasting for 70 years but wondered how much that counted for in the current, very hazardous, economic climate. He said that he thought that Price Bailey's 70-year history was important in that it had shown that it could survive through a World War, a post-war recovery and several recessions. It knew how to cope with differing economic backgrounds and was sure that it would survive the current difficulties.

The party was held on Saturday 14 September and the very next day, the large American financial institutions, AIG, Merrill Lynch and Lehman Brothers all collapsed. Stockmarkets round the world plunged in the following week and President George Bush appeared on prime-time television to try and calm everyone down.

Soon everyone was suffering in the recession that ensued but, in spite of the difficulties, Price Bailey managed to keep growing and in the year to March 2009 improved its position in the Top 50 UK Accounting Firms League Table from 40 to 37. Peter Gillman said of this performance:

> I am delighted with our success which is a reflection of our cautious, but balanced, approach to the recession. We thank all of our staff for their commitment which has helped us achieve this result. I am sure a recession is focussing the minds of many firms, but running a regulated organisation, attracting and retaining quality people, maintaining technical standards and looking after clients is crucial but increasingly demanding.

And Price Bailey was still completing major deals for its clients. The first was brought to a conclusion by Trevor Smith, a partner in the Ely office, acting on behalf of clients to raise the finance to acquire 16 caravan parks in Gloucestershire. The second was achieved by corporate finance partner, Lawrence Bailey, who acted on behalf of clients who wanted to retire and sell their two specialist care homes. Bailey said of the two transactions,

> These transactions indicate that it is still possible to bring deals to a conclusion even in this difficult environment. Both businesses are extremely successful but it is perhaps no coincidence that both transactions are underwritten by value in the freehold property.

Trevor Smith – still doing deals for Price Bailey in spite of the post-2008 recession.

10 | Renewed expansion

UK Large firm of the year
'Thank you, Bishop's Stortford'
Challenging times ahead

UK LARGE FIRM OF THE YEAR

In the autumn of 2010 Price Bailey was delighted to hear that it had been nominated for the award of 'Large Firm of the Year' in the *Accountancy Age* 2010 Awards, the winner to be announced at the Awards dinner on 17 November.

They were even more delighted when it was announced at the dinner that they were, indeed, the winner. Managing Director, Peter Gillman said:

> It is a great honour to win what is regarded as the premier award for our profession and it is a tremendous compliment to our entire team for their skills,

Charles Olley and Peter Gillman with the trophy after Price Bailey won the 'Large Firm of the Year' in the Accountancy Age *2010 Awards.*

dedication and personality that they bring to the firm. It is wonderful for everyone to receive this recognition from others.

Helping them win the award was growth in the previous twelve months, despite the recession, of 6.8 per cent to £15.7 million with profits per partner rising 9 per cent to £185,000. There were no recession-based redundancies.

With total fee income up to £15.7 million, the firm moved up to 36th place in the Top 50 Accountancy Firms League Table.

In its application for the *Accountancy Age* Award, Price Bailey said this about itself:

How the firm has developed its structure:
In 2008, we celebrated our 70th anniversary. In that time we have grown to have 200 people and over 6,000 clients. By March 2009 year we are budgeting to grow to £15m annual fee income. We have ambitions to double to £30m in the next five years and to be 'world class' within our sectors.

We were among the first of the larger UK practices to adopt the limited liability status and took the opportunity to create a new management structure. Our board of directors and managing director have a constitution giving them the ability to run the firm within a three year electoral and five year planning cycle. This allowed us to create and implement faster strategic changes.

The most dramatic of these has been creating practice-wide departments; abandoning geographic management. This created teams focussed on the different needs of our core client groups; corporate, small business and private client. Our specialists then joined our consulting department and operate across the client based teams.

The structure has great client benefits. By concentrating on a narrower range of client activities, we have improved quality; are able to share people and resources more effectively; have a consistent offer and approach for clients across the whole firm. Clients love it, the feedback is great.

Improved effectiveness and innovation:
The creation of departments; a Managing Director who has three direct reports rather than six, and a board that concentrated on strategic and whole firm issues has fundamentally improved the motivation, productivity and efficiency of the practice. Confidence levels are best reflected by the success rate of the corporate team achieving a 66% gain on new business pitches in the financial year to March 2008. Comparison of the teams is transparent, difficult scenarios can be shared benefiting both staff and clients as the knowledge bank grows. It is easier to refine tasks as there is less bureaucracy leading to clarity of purpose.

Howard Sears with the trophy.

Financial Improvements:

Of significance: Gross Income up 14%, Net Profit up 16% and Profit Per Equity Partner up 12.3%. This is a direct result of restructuring. The firm is on target to reach its goal of £15m fee income for the current financial year. An increase of 30.4% in two years.

Improvements in effective use of resources:

The team now regard themselves as being part of a department first and location second. There are no hidden local agendas, staff retention has improved and career aspirations are more readily achievable. We can, for example, now offer trainees a City seat at our new offices next to Liverpool Street station. The greater willingness to share people across the practice is a direct result of performance being measured by department, not by location. The revised business model has changed the supporting functions creating central teams servicing our network. Marketing and Business Development is more focussed delivering practical and strategic solutions to teams rather than to six offices. A recent telesales campaign targeted at Commercial Property Developers, with a turnover over £5m selling the strength of our team of property experts, produced over 15 appointments. This was from an initial list of 260. We now have strength in depth.

Evidence of winning new clients:

Historically we have achieved reasonable success in gaining new business. However we did not have control over this important area. We could not predict growth and could not switch on the process when needed. Alongside the restructuring a comprehensive plan was agreed resulting in 12% organic growth, knowing where our new business opportunities were, how much was in the pipeline and what is likely to convert over the next three to six months. In the year to March 2008 we recorded £5m of new opportunities with existing and new clients; £3m has been converted with £2m still undecided. How did we achieve this? A board member with specific skills in sales and marketing was given the responsibility of driving through a new sales based program placing those people who wanted it in a business development role. We worked closely with our training partner to create an intense tailor made solution. The process culminated in assessment days, mixing live action assisted sales sessions with written papers. We emphasised 'Value for All' in the sale process, this led to a very professional approach to new business overcoming a lot of in built resistance to 'sell'. The team are highly motivated and relaxed.

Unique services for clients:

- Joint venture with Kester Cunningham John (solicitors). We provide financial planning advice to their clients.
- Within our consultancy wing we have an Employee Consulting team providing clients with the unusual mix of tax, HR and financial advice. The team also carries out pay benchmarking exercises for clients which is unusual for a firm of our size.
- We are environmentally friendly. We have a project with Eon, our energy supplier, to reduce carbon emissions. Our Cambridge office is the guinea pig. This was the subject of a BBC breakfast TV interview with our Managing Director in July. The project is set to run over the coming year.
- Specialist knowledge with LLP conversions, PPR and partner award programs.
- AIM and Plus listings work – quite unique for our size, especially the volume we are involved with.
- Outsourced credit control facility.
- Active on offering and undertaking Assurance report work.

BEST PRACTICE – CONSISTENCY
– CONTINUOUS IMPROVEMENT – VALUE TO ALL

Price Bailey backed up its application with the previous five years' numbers.

Profit and Loss Account

	2007/8	2006/7	2005/6	2004/5	2003/4
	£000	£000	£000	£000	£000
Net Fees	13,071	11,499	11,607	11,175	10,716
Operating Costs					
Staff costs	(5,678)	(5,068)	(4,686)	(4,741)	(4,838)
Depreciation and amortisation	(511)	(517)	(537)	(599)	(582)
Other operating charges	(3,452)	(2,930)	(2,750)	(3,063)	(3,158)
Operating profit	3,430	2,984	3,634	2,772	2,138
Interest payable	(170)	(112)	(117)	(172)	(128)
Profit before tax	3,260	2,872	3,517	2,600	2,010
Tax	(26)	(25)	(76)	(8)	–
Minority and other prior interests	(84)	(62)	–	(8)	8
Profit after tax	3,150	2,785	3,441	2,584	2,018
Average profit per equity member	164	146	161	103	81

Balance sheet

	2008	2007	2006	2005	2004
	£000	£000	£000	£000	£000
Tangible assets	1,376	1,173	1,105	1,044	1,092
Intangible assets	1,015	315	372	621	688
Debtors	4,880	3,939	3,653	3,994	4,127
Cash at bank	491	408	500	184	161
Creditors due within one year	(3,802)	(3,235)	(2,281)	(2,753)	(3,109)
Creditors due after one year	(1,048)	(409)	(716)	(992)	(1,083)
Provisions	(284)	(235)	(280)	(387)	(217)
Net assets attributable to members	2,628	1,956	2,353	1,711	1,659
Minority interests	9	1	2	2	2
Loans and other debts due to members	358	387	619	197	55
Member shares	1,607	1,267	1,259	1,259	1,222
Other reserves	654	301	473	253	380
Total members interests	2,628	1,956	2,353	1,711	1,659

'THANK YOU, BISHOP'S STORTFORD'

And Peter Gillman did not omit thanking the original home of Price Bailey, Bishop's Stortford. A large billboard was erected at the railway station in the town with photographs of Gillman and the *Accountancy Age* award and with:

Thank you
Bishop's Stortford
We couldn't have done it without you!

Gillman maintained that the success, even in London and Guernsey, had its roots in Bishop's Stortford and said:

We like to be plain-speaking and avoid jargon, we like to be up-front about costs and service standards, and we like to be easy people to work with. We also try to avoid taking ourselves too seriously – we really enjoy working with our clients.

That approach reflects the business people in Stortford, Harlow and surrounding area, and we've taken those same principles to places like the City of London and it's worked very well.

We really like our Causeway House location and its prominent position in the town. We're proud to be a Stortford-based business and look forward to many more years associated with the town where it all started.

That is why we say, 'Thank you, Bishop's Stortford!'

A very long-established Bishop's Stortford firm which had benefited from Price Bailey's service for decades was Daniel Robinson & Sons. Established in 1892 the family firm had built itself during the twentieth century concentrating on construction and funeral direction. Following the appointment of the current Managing Director, Gary Neill in the early 1990s, Daniel Robinson grew strongly and Neill is full of praise for the service he has received from Price Bailey and for their help with his charity fund-raising activities.

In commenting on the *Accountancy Age* Award, *Yahoo Finance* wrote:

Despite the recession, the firm has flourished and this year grew 6.8% to GBP 15.7m but that is just part of the story.

Internal communication has been improved with an 'Adding Value Guide' made available to staff through the intranet that also includes a wiki facility, allowing anybody to add articles, insert comments and amend existing materials to keep it up to date.

A few years ago the firm changed their approach of the team towards client relationships by introducing partner contact time and fixed fee levels which helps to deliver a better service through regular contact by the client and accountant at no extra cost.

Price Bailey opened an office in Guernsey, which not only generates income from Guernsey but also facilitates a link to UK clients and creates fees from work

Bartram Robinson and Gary Neill of Daniel Robinson, a long-established client of Price Bailey in Bishop's Stortford.

that would previously have been outsourced. Due to their success in the City of London, earlier this year the practice expanded by moving into bigger premises in Dashwood House.

Offices have been upgraded and departmental structures radically changed so that partners and staff are moved around the practice to where their skills are needed to deliver a premium service to clients, which is clearly widely valued through the feedback they receive from clients.

A new graduate training programme has been implemented, providing structured experience across all departments, enabling newly qualified staff to make an informed decision about career preferences and provide the firm with highly skilled client facing terms for the longer period.

Overall this firm continues to rise to the challenges in what are still difficult economic times for the country.

The *Accountancy Age* 'Large Firm of the Year Award 2010' award was not the only award Price Bailey has received in the last three years. Others were:

- The '*InterContinental Finance* Magazine 2012 Continent Awards' are designed to celebrate firms that have not only survived but flourished during the past 12 months of the recession.

- The '*Lawyers World* Global Awards 2011' recognises leading professional firms across the globe that have performed to exceptional levels despite difficult financial times.

- 'Sage Circle of Excellence Winner 2011' was awarded by Sage in recognition of outstanding customer service.

- 'Dealmakers End of Year Awards 2011' was voted by the readership of *Dealmakers Monthly* Magazine.

- '2011 Leading Advisory Firm of the Year UK' by *InterContinental Finance* Magazine Law Awards.

- 'Top 25 Accountancy Firms 2011' by the influential *Private Client Practitioner* magazine – for the third year running.

- The Leading Adviser Business Award at the Aberdeen UK Platform Awards in 2012.

- Winner of the *InterContinental Finance* Global Awards 2013 that highlight the premier firms that have been nominated and voted as THE BEST in 2013.

- Winner of the *InterContinental Finance* Global Awards 2012 End of Year Country Awards that highlight the premier firms that have been nominated and voted as THE BEST in 2012.

- Shortlisted for the Best Employer category at the British Accountancy Awards 2012.

- Finalist in the Financial Advice Supplier of the Year category in the General Practice Awards 2012.

- UK Specialised Client Audit Provider of the Year and UK Corporate Adviser of the Year in the *InterContinental Finance* Magazine Global awards.

- ACQ Global Awards 2012 – UK financial Adviser of the Year, presented by *ACQ Finance* Magazine.

- UK Private Client Tax Advisory Firm of the Year 2012 in the *Acquisition International* M & A Awards in recognition of the team's growth in a time of economic uncertainty.

CHALLENGING TIMES AHEAD

Peter Gillman was not complacent about Price Bailey's winning of the *Accountancy Age* Award. Seeing '*changing times ahead*' he said:

Recently, I was talking to the managing partner of a small but growing account-ancy firm who very kindly said that they modelled themselves on Price Bailey. He speculated on how long it might take them to build a practice like ours – I said around 75 years!

For all the changes that we have been through in the past six or so years, our recent recognition as UK Large Firm of the Year in the *Accountancy Age* Awards owes a lot to our heritage and the people that shaped the firm over our near 75 year history.

I recently passed 40 years' service with Price Bailey and have seen many changes in the firm and our business community and it is the knowledge that the firm has experienced pretty much everything that can happen in business that gives us the confidence and courage to not only survive but prosper.

It is truly exciting to note how we have evolved from a small firm in a market town into one with thriving regional, London and Guernsey offices and a growing international reputation.

There is no secret to surviving and prospering and humility and caution have a big part to play, but for any business, not just Price Bailey, there are a few rules such as:

- Be strategic and plan ahead
- Be bold, but only after research, more research and a bit more research
- Cash ultimately decides if a business survives and prospers
- Manage effectively what you can control
- With care and forethought even the most difficult tasks can be achieved

More than anything it is looking after the business you have got – our clients are everything. Our success is a direct result of our client's success and client care will always be at the heart of our strategy.

We have ambitious plans for the period ahead and the only certainty is that it will not pan out exactly as we plan – we will manage strategically, but also react to a changing landscape.

Many of the recent changes we have managed in our governance, office and management structures, recruitment and acquisitions were planned, but much was not and was the consequence of the market place and opportunities that came our way.

We certainly did not predict the worst recession in a generation, but we are managing our way through it and have continued to grow and avoid the redundancies that have hit other accountancy firms so hard.

It is not easy and we don't get everything right all of the time, but it is terrific to lead a business with great people and great clients and to now be recognised as the UK Large Firm of the Year really is the icing on the cake.

11 | The world's our oyster

GUERNSEY FIRST THEN WHERE?

Martin Clapson became Chairman of the Price Bailey Management Board when Colin Long retired. He felt that Price Bailey should grow internationally. The firm was receiving queries increasingly with regard to Europe and the USA and, after making some enquiries, Clapson felt that Price Bailey should join the International Association of Professional Accountants (IAPA). Before that expansion he, along with Peter Gillman, felt they should open an office in the City of London, and we have seen how that was achieved.

At the Berlin conference of IAPA in 2007, where he spoke on Business Strategy, Clapson met Colin Pickard, the partner of an accountancy firm in Guernsey. Pickard told Clapson – and other UK firms – that he had so much business he was struggling to cope.

Clapson offered to lend him two of the Price Bailey staff, and, two years later, carried out a feasibility study of opening a Price Bailey office in Guernsey.

Guernsey was the second largest of the Channel Islands after Jersey. The language was English and the island had enjoyed centuries of political stability and good governance. The British crown retained the rights over foreign affairs and defence and, although Guernsey was not part of the European Union it had the right to the free movement of goods and trade. It was also a low tax jurisdiction in 2007. There was no capital gains tax, inheritance tax, estate duty, VAT or Stamp Duty. Corporation Tax on company profits was zero except for banks where it was only 10 per cent. Income tax for Guernsey residents was 20 per cent on their Guernsey income while for non-Guernsey income it was capped at £250,000.

In Guernsey the population was 65,726 in July 2008, a working population of 32,834 while unemployment at 232 was negligible. Gross Domestic Product at £1.666 billion in June 2007 had shown a 64 per cent growth over the £1.016 billion in 1998. The main industries were tourism and finance with

Aerial view of Guernsey. (Works in Print/Don McCrae)

finance accounting for 23 per cent of the island's employment and 55 per cent of its Gross Domestic Product.

In December 2007 there were 47 licensed banks with £119 billion of deposits, an increase of 29 per cent over 2006. There were 623 insurance operations licensed to write insurance business, 149 full and 54 personal fiduciary licences and 30 accountancy firms, although most of them did not do audit work.

Why were Martin Clapson and other partners excited by Guernsey?

It was a growing market with significant fee and profit potential. It would complement the City office and raise the firm's profile, providing a new route to High Net Worth individuals. Furthermore, as opposed to opening an office in another East Anglian market town, Guernsey would bring international links, a new niche market, geographical diversity, fast growth potential. As we have already seen, Guernsey was also a low tax jurisdiction on a different economic cycle from East Anglia. It enjoyed direct links with the City of London.

Boats in St Peter Port, Guernsey. (Works in Print/Don McCrae)

The advantage of Guernsey over Jersey which was, after all, twice as big, was Martin Clapson's growing friendship with Colin Pickard. This made a merger with Colin Pickard and Co. a possibility and would make Price Bailey an established player in Guernsey.

In terms of communication, Guernsey airport had been rebuilt between 2002 and 2004 and could handle up to 1.25 million passengers a year (the airport had handled 820,000 passengers in 2007). Direct flights were operated to Stansted, Gatwick, Dublin, Geneva, Paris and Zurich.

Martin Clapson saw great potential to expand Pickard's business by winning more routine business and corporate clients. The expansion of SBT business was felt to have great potential. On top of this, he saw the real opportunity for expansion in the regulated 'Investment Funds' market which would be a new niche market for Price Bailey. The Investment business in Guernsey, known as Collective Investment Funds, had been established in Guernsey for 40 years with

Colin Pickard, who sold his business in Guernsey to Price Bailey.

total funds under management in June 2008 of no less than £154.458 billion. There were 2,800 funds which all needed auditing. Even a small percentage of those would bring significant income.

How sure could Price Bailey be that they would win a percentage of this audit work? Clapson met a number of people including Peter Radford, the managing director of Bordeaux Fiduciaries and Administrators, Paul Meader, the joint managing director of Carozon Capital Management, and Robert Shepherd, the Managing Partner of Ozannes, the largest local firm of solicitors in Guernsey.

Shepherd was a close friend of Colin Pickard and felt Price Bailey would fit in well with them, and suggested that Jersey should follow. Ozannes had opened there and in three years had grown their businesses there enormously.

All the people Clapson spoke to agreed that there was a gap in the accountancy market between the big four and the one-man bands.

Colin Pickard & Company was the obvious way forward. It was a UK200 Group member and also a member of the IAPA which, as we saw above, was how Martin Clapson met Colin Pickard. Pickard was a well-liked and respected member of the Guernsey community. An ex Rotary president of the Guernsey branch, he was an active networker.

Price Bailey did not jump in without further investigation. Martin Clapson visited four times, Peter Gillman twice and Charles Olley once. Three Price Bailey employees worked for a number of weeks at Colin Pickard & Company, generating fees of £78,819.

At the November 2008 partners' conference Clapson received approval to continue negotiations with Colin Pickard. An update was given at the June 2009 conference and the deal was officially concluded on 11 August 2009. Over the following three years income expanded threefold. The forecast turnover for the year to March 2011 was originally £725,000. At the November 2010 conference it was raised to £900,000. For the year to March 2012 it was originally £800,000 and was raised to £1.25 million. By the conference the forecast for the March 2013 was £1.75 million. The challenge from 2012 is to make the business more profitable.

At the same conference the figures were presented which showed the growth of Price Bailey's international business over the previous three years.

In August 2009 Price Bailey opened its first overseas office when it concluded negotiations to acquire Colin Pickard & Company in St Peter Port, Guernsey, a firm which had been operating there for 15 years. Colin Pickard, who would remain a partner with Price Bailey, said:

> I have known Price Bailey for a number of years. We have worked together successfully on a number of assignments and we all felt the time was right for us to cement our relationship with people we know and trust. We will be able to expand the service we offer to clients at home through the Price Bailey network in the City of London and East Anglia.

Martin Clapson, a Price Bailey partner and chairman of the executive board, added:

> We have been providing support to Colin's practice for some time, as well as securing other work directly on the island, which is a very active financial centre.

Kirsty Pettit, a graduate who joined Price Bailey in 2003,
became Director of general practice in the Guernsey office in 2013.

Situated 30 miles west of France's Normandy coast and 75 miles south of Weymouth, England, Guernsey lies in the Gulf of St Malo. There is a large, deep water harbour at St Peter Port. Embracing the nearby islands of Alderney, Herm, Sark, Jethou, Berhou, Lihou and Brecqhow, the total area is 30 square miles and the population, 65,000.

Throughout its history Guernsey has been subjected to invasions from both France and Britain as well as periodic assaults by pirates. At least by the seventeenth and eighteenth centuries, during the British wars with France and Spain, Guernsey shipowners were able to exploit their location, effectively acting as pirates themselves. Indeed, it was the growth of global, maritime trade in the nineteenth century that brought more prosperity, this time legitimately, to the island.

During the First World War Guernsey's allegiance was with Britain and 3,000 men from the island served in the British Expeditionary Force in 1914. During the Second World War the island was occupied by German troops. Some Guernsey people were deported to camps in south west Germany while a concentration camp was built on Alderney and filled with forced labour, mainly from Eastern Europe.

Eventually liberated, normality returned to Guernsey and since the War the island has become prosperous enjoying both a regular tourist trade as well as growth for financial services such as banking, fund management and insurance which now make up no less than 32 per cent of total income. Light tax and death duties make Guernsey a popular off shore finance centre for private equity funds. It has also become popular with wealthy UK citizens.

In reporting on the year in the Guernsey office, Martin Clapson, Head of International Business, was able to report a magnificent growth in fees, up to no less than 79 per cent, from £813,000 to £1,453,000. However, the office was still making a loss.

A significant development was the granting of a full fiduciary licence in October 2010. This is what Clapson said of that development:

> Some of the services our Guernsey Office is now able to offer include the formation and administration of Trusts, Companies, Pension Schemes and LLPs. We are also able to provide consultancy services around governance structures, board effectiveness and other services.
>
> Obtaining a fiduciary license was a significant development for the office, and it also enabled us to acquire the fiduciary business FIFO Trust Limited at the end of June 2011.
>
> Total Fiduciary fee income for the office was £490,000 in 2012. Last year there was no fiduciary income. A Fiduciary profit was made in the year which offset the general practice loss.
>
> We expect the fiduciary income to grow a mixture of organic growth, targeting new jurisdictions and by acquisition.

In April 2012, Paul Martin moved from the Bishop's Stortford Business team to manage the Guernsey office and Clapson said:

> Our Guernsey office has grown so fast that we believed we needed an experienced and established Price Bailey partner to be resident in Guernsey to help manage the

growth, develop the senior management team who we see taking the office forward for the longer term and ensure the General Practice part of the office moves into profits.

STRATEGIC CHANGES

In 2010, in planning for the future Peter Gillman asked the partners and managers, at their conference, certain questions including,

Which of the following strategic changes do you consider have contributed most to Price Bailey's success?

Departmentalisation
Opening in the City of London
Opening in the Channel Islands
Introduction of partner performance management
Conversion to LLP
Introduction of an elected MD and Board
Consolidation into fewer and larger offices
Sales Training and Recording
Introduction of Client Time
Recession Management

There was no doubt which strategic change the partners and managers voted the most successful. 28 per cent said, 'Departmentalisation'. However, 22 per cent said 'Introduction of an elected MD and Board' and 21 per cent said, 'Consolidation into fewer and larger offices'.

In looking to the future, Gillman asked these questions,

Which of the following planned strategic changes do you consider to be most important to maintaining PB's success?

Growth to £30m
Full insolvency service
Embedding AVG and Wiki
Incubator with equity investments
Consistent and efficient processes
Client Extranet/Portal

Control to remain with equity partners
Employee share scheme
Acceptance of external investment
Further development of international work

Here again, there was a clear answer. 40 per cent said, 'Consistent and efficient processes'. Next was 'Growth to £30m' with 21 per cent.

Also, looking into the future, Martin Clapson asked these questions,

Which of the following locations would you like us to open in order to maximise the value to our clients, our business and our profile?

1) Bury St Edmunds
2) Birmingham
3) Oxford
4) Jersey
5) Geneva
6) Singapore
7) New York
8) Sydney
9) Marbella

The answers were more widespread. 25 per cent opted for Singapore, 15 per cent for Jersey, 14 per cent for Geneva, 13 per cent for Bury St Edmunds and 11 per cent for New York and Birmingham. It is interesting to note that nearly two thirds favoured an overseas office.

PRIVATE CLIENT PRACTITIONER

To add to the joy of winning the *Accountancy Age* Award, Price Bailey were delighted to hear in June 2011 that their Private Client department had been chosen as one of the 'Top 25 Accountancy Firms 2011' by the *Private Client Practitioner* magazine. This was an annual ranking that recognised the biggest and best firms giving high-quality advice to wealthy families and individuals.

James King, the partner leading the private client team, said:

It is fabulous to receive this recognition. We pride ourselves on giving a rather unique one-stop service including private financial planning, tax advice and wealth management, all provided by one key adviser who can co-ordinate everything for the client under one roof.

James King had left school in 1989 and gone to work initially at Friends Provident. He joined McIntyre Hudson in Bedford, then the 25th largest accountant in the country and worked throughout the 1990s as a financial services adviser.

In 1998 he was head hunted by Price Bailey and discussed with Lawrence Bailey the idea of adding the financial planning concept to Price Bailey's offerings. They had tried it earlier when Michael Horwood formed a partnership with Chapman How but this had not worked satisfactorily.

James King, leader of the Private Client team at Price Bailey.

James King agreed to join and began to give advice to individual clients of Price Bailey on investments and pensions. He admits he found it tough but in 2002 Price Bailey Financial Planning Ltd was formed. King was appointed Managing Director of this new company and acquired a 15 per cent shareholding. Peter Gillman and Charles Olley sat on the board.

In October 2003 Price Bailey acquired the financial services firm Roberts and Davis and Price Bailey Financial Planning was able to use this influx of new clients to put a strong infrastructure in place. In 2007 Financial Planning and the Tax department were merged and, in that same year, King became a full equity partner in Price Bailey Financial Planning. The Tax and Financial Planning operations became the Private Client department and by 2012 had a turnover of £2.5 million and employed no fewer than 42 people.

King gave an amusing interview after his appointment as a Price Bailey partner, the only non-qualified accountant to be made a full partner in the firm's history. *Inter alia,* he said:

> I am still not sure why they employed me. I think it was because I was working at an accountancy firm that was larger than them. They had been burned in the past on a joint venture with an adviser and there were issues of cultural compatibility, so it was a significant step. They brought me in and dropped me in a room with a computer I couldn't switch on. I ran around like a lunatic for six months, planning mailshots and other ways to promote what we were doing, coming up with a marketing plan. It was slow going and after a year I had brought in around £70,000, largely in packaged investment products which was probably enough to cover costs which basically consisted of my salary.

King maintains that his side of the business, i.e. acting as an adviser, is different from the standard accounting and audit process saying:

> Culturally, advisers tend to be problem solvers whereas accountants tend to be more about process.

Where are we now?

THE CITY OFFICE EXPANDS
THE MOVE INTO LONDON'S WEST END
GROWING BUSINESS NETWORK
INTERNATIONAL AMBITIONS
PROFESSIONALISM AND EXPERIENCE
SERVING REGIONAL, NATIONAL AND INTERNATIONAL CLIENTS

THE CITY OFFICE EXPANDS

On 6 July 2011 Price Bailey acquired the insolvency practitioners, BN Jackson Norton. The original practice that eventually became PB Jackson Norton was founded in 1837. BN Jackson Norton was formed in 1985 and in July 2011 the firm merged with Price Bailey and changed its name to PB Jackson Norton and subsequently, Price Bailey Insolvency and Recovery.

PB Jackson Norton's licensed insolvency practitioners had many years' experience of working with both corporate and individual clients covering a wide range of complex investigative, rescue and turnaround assignments. Now they would be supported by a team of skilled administrators as well as tax, corporate finance, financial services and business strategy specialists from across the Price Bailey Group.

This is what the press release said:

BN Jackson Norton joins accountancy firm Price Bailey
Insolvency practitioners BN Jackson Norton joined the Price Bailey Group on 6th July, trading as PB Jackson Norton LLP, and the agreement brings a new service line to Price Bailey's client offering. BN Jackson Norton's office network will be closed and the team of insolvency and recovery specialists will move into the Price Bailey City of London office in Dashwood House.

Peter Gillman, Managing Director of Price Bailey, says: 'Price Bailey has maintained a steady and healthy growth even during the recession and this joint venture is part of a strategic plan to continue to build on our service offering and strengthen our local presence in London and across East Anglia. Earlier the same week we also acquired a Fiduciary practice to grow our most recently added office in Guernsey. It's an exciting time for the firm and we are pleased to see the PB Jackson Norton team joining us.'

Paul Higley, Head of Insolvency Services at PB Jackson Norton, says 'BN Jackson Norton is a well-known and respected insolvency practice, with roots dating back to 1837. After a few challenging years I'm very pleased that we can continue to service our clients and grow our business, working closely with other professionals, as part of Price Bailey. I'm looking forward to informing our clients and referrers of additional expertise which we now have available to support companies and individuals in financial difficulties and to launching the PB Jackson Norton brand in the market.

THE MOVE INTO LONDON'S WEST END

On 1 October 2011 Price Bailey acquired the accountancy firm, J.M. Shah & Company. Based in Mayfair, in London's fashionable West End since 1979, J.M. Shah and Company was an independent firm of Chartered accountants and business advisers providing compliance services and proactive advice to clients helping them to optimise their personal and business objectives. The firm had one office with one partner and 15 employees offering both compliance and advisory services. It had a long established client base built on an excellent reputation and a personal service.

The press release said:

Accountancy firm J.M. Shah & Company joins the Price Bailey Group
J.M. Shah & Company has been an independent firm of chartered accountants and business advisers with an office in the heart of Mayfair for more than 30 years. Since 1 October 2011 the firm is now part of the Price Bailey Group, trading as J.M. Shah & Company LLP.

The Price Bailey Group has grown considerably in the last year. The firm has shown a strong organic growth during the recession and has recently boosted the expansion further by acquiring a fiduciary business in Guernsey and an insolvency and recovery practice in London. The Mayfair office forms part of a five year strategic plan to grow and develop the practice and is accompanied by a strong recruitment drive at all levels.

Jitu Shah, owner of J.M. Shah & Company LLP, says: 'With a growing portfolio of clients, both local and international, the firm needed to be able to offer a wider range of services and specialist expertise. When I met Peter Gillman and the partners from Price Bailey I knew I'd found the right match to service those needs.

Jitu Shah merged his successful practice with Price Bailey in 2011.

I'm passionate about offering a high quality and personal service to my clients and it's very important to deal with like-minded individuals when you enter into a venture like this. We are planning for a smooth transition and integration into the Price Bailey Group and I expect things to evolve over time rather than present drastic changes to the office or our clients. We are continuing to trade under the J.M. Shah name for now and will be remaining in our office on Old Bond Street.

Peter Gillman, Managing Director of Price Bailey, says: 'We are very pleased to announce this deal and to now have a fantastic office and representation in the West End. Our Mayfair office will become our third in London as we continue to grow the practice. Many of Jitu's clients will directly benefit from our in-house expertise and links to offshore services from our Guernsey office as well as our well-developed private client offering. However, this deal is very much a strategic fit for both parties as J.M. Shah & Company will help to strengthen our international business as well as existing corporate and private sectors.'

One of Jitu Shah's clients was the UK subsidiary of a Caribbean company called Winfresh which sold the bananas produced by the farmers in the Caribbean islands of Dominica, Martinique, St Lucia, St Vincent, the Grenadines and Grenada. The Company also bought in bananas from Barbados and Trinidad and Tobago.

Price Waterhouse was acting for the holding company in the Caribbean while Jitu Shah acted for the UK company. However, with the new resources provided by Price Bailey, Jitu Shah has won the contract to act for the holding company as well.

After a difficult time trying to compete with the vast plantations operated by

Jitu Shah's practice was based in Mayfair in the West End of London, a perfect location. (Works in Print/Don McCrae)

multinationals such as Chiquita and Fyffes in Central America, Winfresh is prospering under the Fairtrade banner. *The Times* reported on 3 March 2012:

> The solution found by the growers in St Lucia and other Windward Islands, Dominica, St Vincent and Grenada was to go entirely Fairtrade. The Windward Islands' export body, Winfresh, says that the switch has been a life-saver. Sainsbury's, its largest customer, switched to 100 per cent fair trade bananas alongside it, becoming, in 2007, the first supermarket to do so.
>
> According to Justin King, Sainsbury's chief executive, 'Five years ago we hoped the effect of Fairtrade would be to help the business kick on to new higher levels. It turns out the effect of Fairtrade has been to save the industry from total devastation.'

GROWING BUSINESS NETWORK

In 2011 Price Bailey moved into London with this concept which they had promoted successfully in East Anglia for a number of years. Nick Mayhew, the partner in charge of business strategy said:

> We have been running the GBN for nearly eight years at venues around the east of England and it is really nice to bring what we have always known to be a really high quality network event to a City of London audience.

The network reaches growing businesses in the SME sector, and gives owners an opportunity for what Nick calls 'deeper networking'. 'We pick a business issue to workshop together and that allows people to really get to know each other's values, solutions and problems. Working like this takes network contacts below the surface and allows people to discern and create better opportunities with each other.'

Club members rate the sessions very highly and business relationships have become very close.

'Over the years we have covered over 100 different topics, building up a wealth of best practice knowledge for members.'

Matt Coward, a tax partner who joined Price Bailey from PKF (now BDO).

INTERNATIONAL AMBITIONS

Having made its first move overseas in opening an office in Guernsey and having opened offices in both the City and West End of London, Price Bailey has plans to increase its business overseas.

This is what it says about its international ambitions:

> Price Bailey is a full service practice that can advise international businesses trading, or wishing to establish a presence, in Guernsey or the UK – as well as UK firms interested in trading abroad. The firm is 'Large firm of the Year' as awarded by *Accountancy Age* and was recently voted one of the 'Top 25 Accountancy Firms 2011' by the influential *Private Client Practitioner* magazine.

Locations
Price Bailey has seven offices including Guernsey, London City, London Mayfair and Bishop's Stortford near Stansted Airport.

International services
Price Bailey offers a full range of compliance and advisory services for overseas businesses and individuals wishing to maximise value and enable their business and investments to grow.

Doing business in the UK
Price Bailey is a full service practice that can advise international businesses trading, or wishing to establish a presence, in the UK.

Doing business in Guernsey
Our Guernsey office offers a complete range of compliance and advisory services to local businesses and international subsidiaries.

We speak many languages
At Price Bailey our partners and staff speak a range of languages apart from English – from Chinese dialects to Polish and Swahili.

IAPA member
The international reach of our fellow IAPA member firms offers instant access to first-hand knowledge of local regulations, culture and customs.

PROFESSIONALISM AND EXPERIENCE

Here are some comments and thanks from impressed and grateful Price Bailey clients:

The Frank Gates Motor Group
The company had been founded in 1920 by Frank Gates and was run by him and then his son, Edward, until it was floated as a public company in the 1950s, albeit still family-controlled. In 1995, it was delisted and split into three parts – a farm run by Edward's daughter, a contract hire firm, run by Edward's cousin, and the Frank Gates Motor Group, run by Edward himself.

Towards the end of the 1990s the company became dissatisfied with the accountancy advice it was receiving and held a beauty parade to select a new accountancy firm. It looked at small, medium and large firms and amongst the medium firms, Price Bailey, led by Peter Gillman, made the most attractive offer and were appointed in 2001. Robin Threadgold, who joined Gates in 2001, confirmed that it has been the most satisfactory arrangement and has worked closely, first with Nick Mayhew and subsequently, with Paul Dearsley.

Grosvenor Technology

The Hertfordshire-based security company Grosvenor Technology Ltd has been sold to the international security specialists Newmark Security Plc for more than £6.8 million.

'Grosvenor has worked with Price Bailey for many years and it never crossed our minds to use anyone else.

As with any deal of this size, there were ups, downs and some hard negotiations along the way.

Paul Dearsley, the Price Bailey partner whose clients include the Frank Gates Group.

In those situations you need to have absolute confidence in your advisers, and the close relationship we have with Price Bailey meant that we always knew we would get a top quality service and the best advice possible'

As part of the same deal, Grosvenor Technology has acquired Newmark's electronic security division, which has relocated from Redhill, in Surrey, to Bishop's Stortford. Both businesses will now be run in tandem by Grosvenor's management team, based at Millars Tree, Southmill Road, Bishop's Stortford.

The move represents the start of an exciting new era for both firms. The deal brings enormous benefits to both businesses, both in terms of efficiencies and new business opportunities.

Although the two companies will continue to trade as separate organisations, their customers and markets will both benefit from synergies gained by partnering Grosvenor Technology with

Newmark's connections to foreign markets and Newmark's experience in distribution will open up fantastic opportunities for Grosvenor.

Mr Blethyn and co-directors, Alan Burgess and Peter Brooks, launched Grosvenor Technology in 1989, specialising in the design and manufacture of sophisticated access control and security management systems. Today, the company employs more than 30 people and turns over in excess of £3 million a year. Its products are installed in over 1,000 locations world-wide and its customers include British Aerospace, BAA and the Metropolitan Police.

Mr Blethyn paid tribute to Price Bailey's corporate finance team for their part in putting together the Newmark deal.

This is what Price Bailey said about an engineering MBO:

We visited the factory, met the team, understood the manufacturing processes and the main business drivers, looked over the figures and suggested a possible deal that we felt could be funded and which was financially viable.

As one of a number of corporate finance teams that were being considered, we were delighted when we were then chosen to advise and lead on this exciting project.

As a first step, we arranged to meet the vendors, a husband and wife team. They were looking to take early retirement and had a very clear view of the sort of deal they were looking for. They were also very keen to allow their managers to take over the company if it could be arranged.

After reviewing their tax position (which involved an immediate gift of shares from the wife to the husband) and revisiting our original suggestions, it became clear that what we had proposed to the managers was spot on. By structuring the deal in a particular way, the vendors would be able to take advantage of a major tax concession whereby they would pay a low rated capital gains tax. This required a complex legal and financial structure to be put in place, followed by a company reorganisation, which needed the support of our tax specialists who helped obtain the necessary HMRC clearances.

The next question to be faced was how to finance the deal. With our help, the management team prepared a business plan looking forward 5 years. There were a number of assumptions that had to made, but the business was strong and the management team were enthusiastic and committed, all of which came through very strongly.

A number of banks were approached. The managers, with our support, made their presentation to the banks and the banks made their presentations to us. One was then chosen as the lead financial partner. The management team now had to choose their solicitor and, on our recommendation, several were seen. The solicitor who was selected turned out to be perfect. He visited the company as requested and at short notice made the legal clearances and paperwork that were required look easy.

During the financial packaging process, it was necessary to review the capital equipment programme. The financiers to the deal also proved to be helpful here and the company have put plans in place for a substantial new capital investment programme, financed on the back of the growth that the company is currently experiencing.

Here are further comments from satisfied Price Bailey clients:

Excellent customer focussed service at no more cost than any other accounting firm. High value for money.

Robin Hepworth
PAS Aviation (International) Ltd

The accessibility, knowledge and understanding of Price Bailey staff make the annual audit a very smooth and efficient process.

Robert Murray, Danzer UK Ltd

Really impressed by the vision and the offering!

Michael D. Frape, Ashton KCJ

Your professionalism and experience, coupled with good humour, has undoubtedly smoothed the way for us through a stressful time.

Linda and Trevor Fagg
Sale of County Shutters Ltd

Price Bailey has helped to sustain our company's fast pace of growth by engaging the team to focus on and prioritise key issues and objectives. The mixture of guidance, challenge and new thinking has helped the team to grow and meet the new demands of the business, which is now really focussed and flying along again.

Tony Windsor
Windsor Waste Management Ltd

Your experience and skills, together with a dedication to get work completed accurately and on time undoubtedly helps our business work more effectively.

Graham McIntosh, Logotron Ltd

Through lots of hand holding we have with the help of Price Bailey restructured our business in a way that ensured we extracted value at the most efficient tax rate.

Steve Pammenter
SP Landscapes and Tree Contractors Ltd

And here are clients that have been served well by Price Bailey:

Oracle Coalfields was a company for whom the specialist team, led by Tony De Martino and Martin Clapson, acted as auditors from its incorporation and as reporting accountants for both the company's listing on the PLUS Market and its successful move to AIM. Shahrukh Khan, CEO of Oracle Coalfields plc, said:

We are delighted by the work done by Price Bailey who have been with us from inception and look forward to working with them as our business progresses.

The listing received national press and television coverage in Pakistan and helped to bring Oracle a step closer to developing an open cast mine which would lead to more power production and help reduce Pakistan's regular power cuts.

On 13 October 2011, *Business Weekly* reported on another large deal on which Price Bailey had played an important part:

1Spatial acquired by Avisen in £4.74m all-share deal
1Spatial, the Cambridge based leader in location based solutions, has been acquired by fellow UK company Avisen plc in an all-share deal that values 1Spatial at £4.74m.

The business was founded as Laser-Scan in 1969 by three academics from Cavendish Laboratories – the Physics department of the University of Cambridge.

Avisen will acquire the entire issued share capital of 1Spatial. The enlarged group will transition to a single 1Spatial brand.

1Spatial shareholders will be entitled to receive 5.761 fully paid new Avisen shares for each share they hold. The deal values each 1Spatial Share at 22.35 pence based on the closing price of 3.88 pence per Avisen share on October 6.

The enlarged group will be led by a management team drawn from the boards of both 1Spatial and Avisen, comprising Steve Berry as non-executive chairman, Marcus Hanke as CEO, Nic Snape as managing director, Claire Milverton as CFO and Dr Mike Sanderson as director of strategic development. The non-executive directors will be Marcus Yeoman and Mark Battles.

Tony De Martino, the Price Bailey Senior Manager who helped
Oracle Coalfields towards their flotation.

Nic Snape, CEO of 1Spatial said: 'Our profile in the spatial industry has never been higher and the access to capital and business acumen that Avisen brings will enable us to capitalise on the foundation we have built from our own resources.

'The 1Spatial board are confident that the combined companies will accelerate the growth of 1Spatial and provide significantly enhanced shareholders' return.'

Price Bailey has acted for 1Spatial for several years including the reverse acquisition and AIM listing of 1Spatial Holdings plc in 2010. So when the opportunity came to combine the activities of 1Spatial into Avisen, the executive directors turned to Price Bailey to provide due diligence on Avisen under a very tight deadline.

Price Bailey's corporate, corporate finance and tax consulting teams worked closely to investigate and review the key issues necessary for the 1Spatial board to complete their decision making and recommendations to their own shareholders on the deal.

The 1Spatial assignment was coordinated by client manager Ben Bullman, supervised by Simon Blake – Price Bailey's lead corporate finance partner – and assisted by Dan Gammon and Victoria Nicoll.

Grays of Cambridge is another well-known Cambridge company that has been served well by Price Bailey. Founded in 1855 by Henry John Gray, the Champion Racquets Player of England and professional at St John's College, the company began by making, stringing and selling racquets and balls. It grew rapidly and soon gained a reputation for the manufacture of high quality sports equipment. Grays continued to grow in the twentieth century and the fifth generation of Grays now run a world famous company manufacturing top quality sports equipment. It also still operates its original retail outlet in Cambridge.

Michael Ellsom of Rollins in Harlow said this of the service his company had received from Price Bailey over the last 40 years:

> We originally operated at Tower Hill in London and used a London accountancy firm. They were constantly raising their fees and when we moved to Hertford in 1970 I asked our bank, the Midland, if they could recommend a new firm. They suggested Price Bailey and first, Richard Price and then Nick Mayhew, organised our audit, ably assisted by Ian Smith. We found them all charming and highly efficient.

SERVING REGIONAL, NATIONAL AND INTERNATIONAL CLIENTS

This is what Price Bailey says about itself in 2012 and why potential clients should become actual clients:

> Price Bailey has three offices in London (City, Mayfair and North London) and offices in Bishop's Stortford, Ely, Cambridge, Norwich and Guernsey. Each office serves local SMEs, private clients and regional, national and international businesses.

> *Award winning – as voted by both the profession and our clients*
> We are proud to have been awarded 'Large Firm of the Year 2010' by *Accountancy Age*, 'Top 25 Accountancy Firms 2011' by the influential *Private Client Practitioner*

Alastair Cook, Captain of the England cricket team, hits a boundary with a Grays of Cambridge bat.

Jonny Wilkinson kicks a drop-goal to win the World Cup for England in 2003 with a Grays of Cambridge Gilbert ball.

magazine, '2011 Leading Advisory Firm of the Year UK' by *InterContinental Finance* Magazine Law Awards, 'Sage Circle of Excellence Winner 2011' by Sage in recognition of outstanding customer service and 'Dealmakers End of Year Awards 2011' as voted by the readership of *Dealmakers Monthly* Magazine.

Client centric

We always ask for client feedback – and usually receive ridiculously good results. 98% of our clients say that they would, or already have, recommended us to others. (Based on more than 1000 feedback forms that our clients have filled in for us during the last five years.)

To learn more about how we achieve this, see below:

- We are organised in cross-practice departments specifically designed for each client segment: business, corporate and private client.
- Our special sector teams also add an additional layer of expertise to our services and strive to offer the best advice possible.
- Our core values are focused on the needs of the client: Value for all, Best Practice, Consistency and Continuous improvement.

Simply very nice people to work with

Our clients most commonly describe us as professional, helpful, approachable and friendly. Our focus on offering a high quality service with professional and straightforward advice is clearly valued by our clients. Here are just two of the comments we really like: 'An excellent local firm with a comforting depth of expertise in international matters.' 'Very efficient, straight talking people with great sense of humour and helpful in every way.'

Price Bailey is already helping a growing and successful client base and we could do the same for you.

The right advice for life

- The firm has a high degree of technical and local business knowledge and invests heavily to stay informed of the latest legislation and accounting practices.
- The firm has superb systems in place to deliver the work on time.
- Teams are able to offer clients advice across a wide range of services to ensure that each client benefits from a joined up approach that adds real value to their business and personal affairs.
- Price Bailey offers fixed fee arrangements, so there are no surprise charges.

In 2011 Price Bailey set up an official graduate training programme and called it STEPSTONE. It reminded some of the partners of the programme initiated by Peter Crouch in the 1980s. It began with: 'Making the Step from Student to Professional', under which it said:

We've dedicated a lot of time to Price Bailey's future, thinking about the direction in which we want to move our business and the individual skills which we need to get us there.

StepStone has been designed to create highly skilled managers, directors and partners of the future, who are not only technically excellent, but who understand and support our vision and services inside and out.

We firmly believe that excellence comes from creating our own professionals from the start and we have tailored our StepStone programme to uphold this.

Our approach to training differs from larger and other medium sized firms, in that we aim to provide our trainees with an all-round accountancy experience. Not only will you have a comprehensive four week induction programme when you begin employment with us, introducing you to our people and our services; but you will also undertake substantial work experience in all areas of our business during the first three years of your training. On top of that, you will also work towards your ICAEW (ACA) qualification to become a chartered accountant.

It went on to say that it was essential that all the different services Price Bailey offered should be understood by all employees. In short, these services were:

Business

The Business Team inform, develop and support SMEs. This can vary from carrying out book-keeping, keeping annual business accounts up to date to filing tax returns accurately and on time.

Corporate

The Corporate Team is in place to support larger businesses. Typically, the team undertake audits, produce financial statements and Abbreviated Accounts and undertake corporate tax compliance work.

Private Client

The Private Client Team help individuals to manage their wealth. This generally involves providing them with financial planning & tax advice.

Consulting

Underpinning all the above services is our consulting team. Made up of technical experts, the consulting team provide advice on business systems and complex tax issues. They also provide guidance on buying & selling businesses & help them to create effective strategies.

It then laid out the step-by-step process by which a graduate would progress from raw recruit through the training to qualification as a chartered accountant so that:

After five years with us, you're likely to know which areas of the business you enjoy and we will be encouraging you to progress within those teams. You may also wish to develop supervisory skills towards a future management role. As well as this, you may choose to hone your skills in specialist areas by taking further qualifications, such as Chartered Tax Adviser (CTA).

The Price Bailey culture was very important to the partners and they laid out to graduates exactly what they felt it to be:

Our Culture

Our culture is all about the way we do things at Price Bailey. We put our clients first, we work hard and we remain professional at all times. We aim to continually improve our knowledge and services, and to be consistent in our approach.

Our Teamwork

We work well as one organisation, despite having seven separate office locations. This is because we have representatives of each of our departments in each location – we hold whole team meetings where we get to meet with others from our teams and we often move around the different offices to work on assignments.

Our Friendliness

We pride ourselves on our friendliness. In fact, in a recent survey, when asked to describe the culture of Price Bailey, 'friendly' came up trumps, followed closely by 'professional'. And a whopping 86% of employees felt they well and truly 'belonged' within Price Bailey, with the remaining 14% stating lack of longevity as the only reason for their negative response.

Our Work-Life Balance

We like to think we have similar professional ethics and attitudes to larger accountancy firms, but we probably offer a better work/life balance. We recognise you have a life outside of work and we encourage you to make the most of it! However, whilst we don't expect you to work 24 hours a day, we do expect you to work hard whilst you are here & you need to be fully committed to undertaking at least three years of study when you first join us – often at the expense of a night down the pub!

Our Generalist Training

Unlike in larger firms who tend to offer experience in one area only, with Price Bailey you are going to get a really strong grounding in accountancy – you'll learn how to number crunch and to produce a set of accounts that balance and make sense. We'll make sure you can do this before you tackle anything else. This skill is becoming rarer by the day & is one we are proud to maintain.

Exposure to Clients

With Price Bailey you will be exposed to a wide range of clients & you will often have direct contact with the business owner – this means you quickly develop the business and communication skills which you require to be successful.

Exercising Influence

Being part of a firm consisting of just over 220 [now almost 300] people, means that you will have the opportunity to exercise influence at an early stage in your career. You are at the heart of where all the decisions are made and your route to decision making yourself is a relatively short one. You will be able to communicate with Partners, Heads of Department and the Managing Director fairly easily – allowing for a much greater sense of identity.

They quoted what Kirsty Pettit, a graduate who had joined Price Bailey in 2003 and had risen to Senior Manager, Business Team, said of her training with the firm,

> I qualified as a Chartered Accountant in 2005 and since then I have undertaken a variety of roles including being seconded to a large law firm in the City to work as their finance manager. In 2008 I moved to the Consulting team and I have been involved in a range of projects both in the Corporate Finance Team and Business Strategy Team. I am working towards my Corporate Finance Diploma and undertaking the Mindshop Accredited Facilitator programme.
>
> I enjoy the buzz of working with different people on different assignments each day. I have the chance to be a part of a crucial decision in a clients' life.

And also two other graduates, Ronan Wade, a Manager on the Business Team, who said:

> Before joining Price Bailey I had completed a degree in Chemistry and spent two years working for a church. Not the most obvious preparation, but I found that if you have a good grasp for figures and are keen to be in accountancy then your background is not important.
>
> I came to accountancy in order to gain an insight into businesses and I haven't been disappointed. I work in our Business team, dealing with small businesses and the self-employed. Through this I see a wide variety of trades and services and have gained a broad knowledge of accounting practices. I also really enjoy being able to work closely with clients, and being able to assist in tangible ways with their work.
>
> I've found Price Bailey a really friendly and relaxed place to work. They provide support and encouragement through studying for professional exams, while also giving you a variety of experience within the practice, which I made the most of having originally started in the audit team. I encourage anyone interested in a career in accountancy to apply to Price Bailey, come ready to work hard, but also to enjoy that work.

And Gerry Tang, now a member of the Audit and Compliance team, who said:

I joined Price Bailey's Business Team having graduated with a degree in Economics. I wanted to join a profession where I would be tested each day and so far I have not been let down.

Despite having only worked with PB for a few months, I have already worked on an extensive range of clients, seeing the work through from the planning stage to completion. I'll have the opportunity to go on a secondment to the Corporate team to further broaden my understanding of accountancy and audit.

I have also returned to college to study for the ACA. Having never studied accountancy before, going back to college to read an unfamiliar subject seemed like a daunting task. However, it's great to see what I learn in class fall into place at work.

From my first interview, it was apparent how open and approachable everybody was. It was undoubtedly the friendliest environment I visited when applying for jobs. I would urge anybody who wants a challenging career with substantial future prospects to apply to join Price Bailey.

Catherine Willshire is Head of Compliance at Price Bailey.

Finally, it laid out *The Golden Rules*, saying:

In every aspect of our work there is some risk, and no matter how hard we try it can **never** be eliminated.

However with a structured common approach, risk will be identified sooner and therefore dealt with better.

The Golden Rules are the essential rules which must be followed by all. We believe, if followed these will mitigate risks and enable a structured common approach to our work.

The Golden Rules
1. Recognise any sign or indication of client dissatisfaction. Never cover up or turn a blind eye, and always refer to an appropriate complaints handler.
2. Know the boundaries within which you are expected to work and your primary objectives.
3. Know and respect the extent to which you are allowed to represent or commit the firm.
4. Be aware of the impact that your actions and decisions have on the reputation and performance of the firm.
5. Always be quick to refer any doubts or concerns about any performance or operating issues to a Partner or member of the RMF.
6. Always follow systems and guidelines set by the firm.

Nadia Khan,
Director of HR at
Price Bailey.

13 | The future

PRICE BAILEY IN 2013

In the Annual Report for the 12 months ended 31 March 2012, Peter Gillman was able to report on a 'busy and successful' year following what he described as a 'disappointing' 2010/11.

In reporting on Corporate Services its Head, Paul Dearsley noted that the fifth year of the department had been a very good one with an operating profit of £927,000 against £615,000 the previous year. There had been some successful new business wins, notably Trevor Smith's large conditional fee for assisting a client with a major acquisition. The department, School Academies, had been created during the year by Gary Miller and Paul Bartlett which brought in £350,000 of new businesses, mainly audits for corporate.

Howard Sears, Business Department Head, was also able to report a 'solid set of results … given a year of extremely tough economic conditions.' On Business Development, Howard said:

> The hard work put in by the business development group over the last eighteen months or so has begun to pay off with new wins which were added to the pipeline some time ago now coming to fruition across our sectors.
>
> In particular we have focussed on healthcare putting together a good quality team, brochures and website. This is now beginning to bring in new work from both NHS GP's, private practitioners and dentists.
>
> Our professional services team continue in the main to work with lawyers and are now assisting many in their conversion to an ABS (Alternative Business Structure).

James King, Head of Private Client, reported a mixed year with a 10 per cent fee growth, but a contribution to central costs and profit down slightly and operating profit also down. On the plus side, the client funds under advice had advanced to nearly £250 million with almost £100 million of that under active management. He concluded:

> We continue to offer our three core services of Discretionary Management, Advisory and Employee Benefits and within those we provide investment management, financial planning, protection, capital and income taxes advice and compliance, and lifestyle planning. We believe this is one of the most comprehensive offerings available from a single source and we continue to promote this strongly as our USP. It puts us in a very strong position to demonstrate RDR readiness.
>
> We have relocated most of the City private client team to Mayfair to help absorb some of the high workload there and to take advantage of the many new opportunities that are coming our way.
>
> As I write this the macro economic factors affecting Europe are having an adverse impact on markets generally and no doubt on our clients' financial confidence. However I remain optimistic that we can continue to advise them sensibly and that our business will not be seriously damaged by short term market difficulties.

The Consulting team partners – Simon Blake on corporate finance, Charles Olley on tax, Nick Mayhew on business strategy and systems, and Tony Sanderson on insolvency and recovery – reported a tough year. Insolvency and recovery was the latest of specialist consulting services offered by Price Bailey and, as we have seen, came about through the acquisition of BN Jackson Norton in July 2011. The name was changed to Price Bailey Insolvency and Recovery to take advantage of the Price Bailey brand.

THE MAYFAIR OFFICE

As we have also seen, during the year the business of J.M. Shah and Company LLP was acquired and Jitu Shah said this of the merger:

> I was delighted that we were able to agree terms for my colleagues and I to join Price Bailey in October 2011. Mayfair has been a great place for us for many years. We had developed a successful practice and had grown beyond what we

could deliver on our own, arriving at a juncture where we were in need of a wider range of specialist services to take the business forward and service our clients to a fuller extent. Price Bailey was the perfect fit for our firm and I hope that in due course the mutual trust and benefit from this transaction will be felt by the partners, employees and our clients.

The Mayfair office provides a broad range of audit, accounting, outsourcing and tax services to local business and to the internationally mobile. We aim to offer a one stop shop for our clients and leave them free to concentrate on major

Gary Miller joined Price Bailey as a partner from BDO Stoy Hayward in 2008.

business decisions without the anxiety of complex compliance, especially when cross border matters are involved.

We will continue to attract international business through our excellent reputation and concentrate business development activities in particular regions. We have a diverse, multi lingual office with close global connections. We look forward to working with Price Bailey's established international connections to enhance our services both for inward and outward investment.

Some benefits of becoming part of Price Bailcy are already apparent, as existing clients with sophisticated needs feel able to refer more work to us.

We have adopted a much required staggered approach to the merger, retaining our pre-merger trading style of J.M. Shah & Company and preferring to assure and retain clients and our team than impose any rigid adherence to the established Price Bailey procedures. That said, we have now started down the road to integration as our teams start to work together and we are pleased to welcome senior representatives of all parts of Price Bailey into the office, some now permanently based here, others as needs demand.

Financially, despite the distractions of change, we have delivered more than expected. Gross income for the first six months with Price Bailey exceeded expectations at £823,000 and we made a significant contribution of £163,000 to central overheads, amortisation and profit.

IAPA

Price Bailey became a full member of the International Association of Professional Accountants (IAPA) on 1 January 2010, and this is what Clapson said about Price Bailey's membership:

IAPA is a global association of independent accountancy and business advisory firms who provide accounting, audit, tax advisory and business consultancy services.

Price Bailey joined as full members on 1 January 2010 and since then Simon Blake and I have attended conferences, to raise the profile of Price Bailey. IAPA has over 220 member firms with offices in 60 countries. The association is one of the top 25 global accounting associations with annual income of over 1 billion US$. IAPA is growing rapidly and was recently shortlisted for the 2012 International Accounting Bulletin award 'Rising Star Association'.

There are a number of UK member firms, with one UK member firm bigger than us. Simon and I always offer to present and be active at all the conferences

Simon Blake – Price Bailey's Corporate Finance partner.

we attend. The aim is to be the 'UK preferred firm' with IAPA. I have facilitated business strategy sessions at conferences in Moscow and Montreal and Simon has also provided updates on European initiatives in respect of Corporate Finance. Our sessions are always well received.

The opportunities, work flow and referrals in and out of Price Bailey have continued to grow over time. We should not forget we have only been full members for just over two years and the activity to date is encouraging.

I have been asked to join the European Board of IAPA at this year's European Conference AGM. I was pleased to accept and this can only help to increase our profile internationally and move us closer to the aim of being the 'UK preferred firm' with IAPA. [Martin Clapson became Chairman of the European Board of IAPA in 2013.]

With our raising profile within IAPA, we continue to see our Guernsey office and our new Mayfair office, which has a strong international bias, as a springboard for more international work. City of London, Mayfair and Guernsey linked in with our full membership of IAPA, is a strong foundation for our international business to grow.

Already in 2012 we have performed audit work in the Caribbean and Pakistan. We have had a qualified Egyptian partner working with us in the UK, to learn how we do things at Price Bailey. We have been appointed to help an Australian company list on the Frankfurt stock exchange. All happened since 1 January 2012. We are becoming international!!

THE STRATEGIC PLAN

Price Bailey has recruited a number of new partners over the last five years and they all expressed great enthusiasm about the firm and its future.

Gary Miller had worked at Price Waterhouse in the 1970s and early 1980s before becoming a partner at Finney & Co. in Chelmsford where there were 40 partners. Finney & Co. merged with Stoy Hayward who became BDO Stoy Hayward with 300 partners. Miller said that he had always been aware of Price Bailey and remembered losing out to Martin Clapson on a pitch in 2005. He was introduced to Peter Gillman by Tony Sanderson and was delighted to be invited to join the firm in 2009. He said later: 'I have been given the freedom to work in the way I thought best and am extremely glad that I made the move.'

Daren Moore had a similar experience, working his way up Baker Tilly with its 270 partners. He too has enjoyed the flexibility at Price Bailey and feels that the departmentalisation was a very important development.

Another new partner, Aaron Widdows, who joined Price Bailey from PKF, now BDO, in June 2010, and who works in the Corporate Team, also likes the flexibility rather than all policies being driven by a London head office which was his previous experience.

Tony Pennison, who had joined in 1997 as an assistant manager and became a partner in 2012 agreed with Gary Miller, saying: 'I love the variety of working in the Business Team.'

Peter Gillman pointed out that Price Bailey had changed immensely over the past five years and particularly in the last year. For example, fees in 2010 had amounted to £15 million while he expected them to be over £21 million in the year to March 2013. 'We are now a UK Top 30 firm and it was only in 2008 that we hit the Top 40'.

Tony Sanderson, a partner whose specialities include insolvency and recovery.

The number of employees had grown from 200 a few years earlier to 300. New services – insolvency and fiduciary – were now being offered, and a new office had been opened in London. Furthermore, 'we are now a leading adviser to law firms and school academies and our audit work takes us to such diverse places as Asia and the Caribbean.'

In putting forward a *Strategic Plan*, Gillman said:

We were of course UK Large Firm of the Year in 2010 and that marked the completion of our old development plan – essentially inwardly focussed. The next

Daren Moore, a partner who joined Price Bailey from Baker Tilly,
feels the departmentalisation is a very important development.

part of the plan is to grow our business significantly and broaden our services alongside service improvements to world class standards. The changes noted reflect this current plan and are a controlled development of our business in order to maximise the market position we have created and build a sustainable and independent firm for the long term.

We are on track – we have been bold without being reckless. We know that many other UK firms are not doing so well and are struggling to cope with the economic uncertainly and with that are contracting and making redundancies. Our business

Aaron Widdows, a partner who enjoys the flexibility of the Price Bailey approach.

has changed significantly, but it had to or we might have been faced with the same downward trend.

We will be more complex – more departments, more international work, a new office, new services with new risks.

We will create more opportunities and have seen several recent promotions to partner, director and senior manager levels. But we still need to develop more

Tony Pennison, who became a partner of Price Bailey in 2012,
agreed with Gary Miller about the variety of work at Price Bailey.

partners and senior personnel in response to our growth and replace those that will naturally retire in the next few years. We want at least half of those appointments and possibly more to be internal promotions.

Management Teams – We have created more effective functional management teams to suit the larger and more complex business and this is particularly evident in HR and Marketing.

Career Development – We will shortly introduce a new career development initiative designed to support and challenge everyone seeking promotion from newly qualified through to partner level.

Technology – We plan to invest more in technology not only to improve the functionality of our systems, but to introduce new facilities in such areas as mobile working and client relationship management.

PR and Communication – We wish to raise our public profile and improve in all forms of communication both internal and external so that we maximise our success stories and create a much wider awareness of Price Bailey as one of the leading brands in our profession.

ABS STATUS

In April 2013, Price Bailey learnt, to its delight, that it was the first accountancy firm in the UK to be granted an alternative business structure (ABS) licence. This meant that the new legal entity, Price Bailey Legal Services LLP, was now licensed to undertake a number of reserved legal activities ranging from probate services, rights of audience, conduct of litigation, reserved instrument activities and the administration of oaths.

Peter Gillman said:

Once the legislation came in it has been something of a discussion topic between lawyers and accountants as to whether there is a movement in the market to bring the two professions together. The logic of an allegiance is clear to see.

However, Gillman made it clear that Price Bailey would not be treading on the toes of its legal clients.

WHERE WILL WE BE IN 2015?

The then Managing Director, Peter Gillman, laid out clearly Price Bailey's plan for the coming three years:

The Board follows a five year plan to guide the development of the business in the medium term. The plan may be briefly summarised as follows,

Vision

We will be a world class firm, with a national reputation and global connections.

We have always believed Price Bailey to be a great firm with great people and, although we do well, we are only now beginning to live up to the full potential that we believe we can achieve together.

By 2015 we not only want to reach that full potential, but go beyond. To do this we need to focus on creating value for every client.

Values

- Best Practice
- Consistency
- Continuous improvements
- Value to all

This means:

- to focus on clients in terms of what they want and how they want it delivered

- taking the best of what we do and implementing it throughout the practice

- keeping a close eye on useful developments in our industry that might be of value to our clients and team

- ensuring that the style and quality of service throughout our business is at consistently high levels

- to do things the best way, but also the same way so that our clients and teams can enter any part of Price Bailey and feel they are in the same firm and a great one

- to actively look for opportunities to improve things and have a system that reviews and adopts improvements across the firm

- taking the best examples of client service that we see and training our teams to deliver the service across the whole firm

- and finally to hold 'Value to All' at the core to our actions and challenge our working practices always to show value to our clients, our people, our contacts and our suppliers

We are already one of the most capable firms in the UK. By 2015 there will be no question in anyone's mind what we stand for and how we do things. We will be world class, with a national reputation and global connections.

Price Bailey's City office, 2012.

Fees

We will design and plan for fees of £30m per annum without inflation but including acquisitions.

Growth has been good over the last few years and continued through the recession. A growing practice is essential for:

- providing opportunities for promotion and development of key team members

- attracting talented new people to the practice

- refreshing the client base

The firm has a clear understanding of how to generate new business and plan and execute this consistently. Growth rates will exceed those we have seen recently.

Our sustainable profitability

We will design and plan our business to increase the underlying net profit to turnover ratio by 1.5% per annum.

Our services

We will maintain our focus on meeting clients' core needs, but develop consulting, insolvency and incubator services to broaden our offering. We will give greater emphasis to developing international services.

Our clients

We will improve the average client grading to 'B', and ensure a clear understanding of service requirements and delivery.

Our people

We will build around general practitioners, with appropriate sector specialisms and recognised expertise. We will focus on contact with clients and meeting their needs. We will provide clear role definitions and expectations, professional training and career development and effective performance appraisal.

Our processes

We will be focused on identifying the different needs of our clients and matching our offering to fulfil those needs. Our business offering will be consistent and franchisable, yet always improving and with appropriate use of technology at its heart.

Our locations

The office network needs to be sufficient to serve the needs of our clients, both in the UK and overseas.

Our capital

We will retain capital in the business to finance growth generally and enable us to take those opportunities that meet our investment and acquisition criteria.

Ownership

Control will remain with partners, but by 2015 we will be attractive to external investors. A real business, not just a place to work.

We should end this book with some words from the retiring Managing Director and now Executive Chairman, Peter Gillman:

The idea to create a book recalling the history of Price Bailey was prompted by the 75th anniversary of the founding of our firm. The next major milestone would be our centenary in 2038 and with the best will in the world, it would be most unlikely that many of those that were around in the earlier years would still be with us and able to assist in the creation of a book such as this.

Consequently, this became a unique opportunity to create a history of the firm with direct access to many of those that have contributed to the Price Bailey story. 2013 became the target date for publication and it is a matter of some coincidence that 2013 also marks a staging post in the executive management of our firm.

After twelve years, first as Managing Partner and then our first Managing Director, I am to become our Executive Chairman and Martin Clapson has been appointed to succeed me as Managing Director. The changes also see the retirement of Richard Price, our Non-Executive Chairman, and with Richard finally leaving the firm after 45 years' service and, as a result, we sever the last direct link with our founding partners, Richard being the son of Stanley Price.

These are therefore significant times for our firm and inevitably a time for reflection both in where we have come from and where we are going. But why is a long history of achievement important in a modern and ever changing business world?

I think it is very important in two respects:

First it is that history and the people that created it that set the tone of our personality, values and ambition.

Second, it demonstrates the ability of an organisation to adapt, take advantage of opportunities, deal with crises and create a sustainable future.

Helena Wilkinson, who joined Price Bailey as a partner from
Chantrey Vellacott in August 2013 and will head
the Not for Profit sector which covers charities.

Many might think that the 21st century is unprecedented in the pace of change and the uncertainty that seems to dominate our business and personal lives. But how different is it really from the year the firm was founded, 1938?

What must it have felt like back then with the world on the brink of what became a huge conflict where the sovereignty of many countries was at serious risk of historic change? The very real fear of a fascist-led dictatorship would surely have dominated everyone's thinking when our predecessors set up Price Bailey.

So maybe our history is very important to our future – a long history does demonstrate the resilience of a business and that perhaps goes deeper than simply being good at management.

I believe it goes to the root of what a business is about – its values and its people that subscribe to those values. If those values are maintained by people that truly believe in them, then maybe that is what makes the business able to cope with pretty much anything.

Our 'official' values are stated in our strategic plan – Best Practice, Consistency, Constant Improvement and Value to All – and they are very important to our development and achieving our strategic goals.

But I believe our 'soft' values are at the heart of what our firm is really about and define the look and feel of what we are trying to achieve and I would wager that those same values were present in 1938 and every year since.

What are they? I think they are:

- nice people to deal with
- clever
- unpretentious
- humble
- honest
- not taking ourselves too seriously
- caring

These are the values you can't dress up in fancy words and a glossy brochure. These are words that describe what it feels like to walk into one of our offices or pick up the phone to one of my colleagues.

These are the words that explain why people want to come and work with us and why those that already work for us want to stay and develop their careers with us. They are also why clients want us to be their advisers and why they recommend others to use us as well. This is also why our suppliers think we are great customers to have.

However, let me add that we are not perfect and we do sometimes get things wrong. But on the rare occasions that we do, our commitment to sorting things out is a further demonstration of our values.

When I hear a colleague say 'I'm Price Bailey through and through' or when a client says 'It doesn't matter who you talk to at Price Bailey, they all want to be so helpful' – that is our values in action.

If those values define us and we can confidently maintain them, then surely that 75-year history can be extended to many further chapters in the future. It is fascinating to consider what the future might hold for Price Bailey. If our predecessors might be amazed to learn that the business they started would now be ranked in the Top 30 in the UK and would have been awarded the UK Large Firm of the Year in 2010, then I suspect we would be equally amazed to discover what Price Bailey might be like in 2088 – 75 years' time.

Just as it would have been fanciful 75 years ago to imagine 2013, so it would be to try and have the remotest clue what 2088 will look like.

However, what I can say is that with continued good management (and we have a raft of very capable people coming through to take up those future responsibilities) the right decisions will be made in the coming years for our people and our clients.

That could mean Price Bailey remaining as an independent business as we currently plan or it might see something very different. What I can predict is that our firm will continue to develop our multi-cultural and diverse work force and client base, our London presence and our International profile. I also hope that this can be achieved whilst retaining our regional roots and way of doing business.

The key to good management is dealing with present challenges, reacting to new ones and having a strategic plan for the immediate future that is predictable. If those disciplines are maintained then we can be confident that whatever 2088 looks like or indeed the years up until then, we will run our business successfully for the benefit of our people and our clients.

I hope you have found our story an interesting one but, more than anything, I hope within it you have seen why we have been around so long and why we plan to be around for a long time to come.

Appendix 1

Price Bailey Partners

		Current	Former	Deceased
1	Leslie Benten			Leslie Benten
2	Stanley Price			Stanley Price
3	Reginald Bailey			Reginald Bailey
4	Alan Deighton			Alan Deighton
5	Don Holledge			Don Holledge
6	Stan Trow			Stan Trow
7	Vernon Clarke			Vernon Clarke
8	Norman Hall			Norman Hall
9	Graham Hardy		Graham Hardy	
10	Graham Savage		Graham Savage	
11	Michael Horwood		Michael Horwood	
12	Richard Price		Richard Price	
13	Roger Evans		Roger Evans	
14	Nigel Bailey		Nigel Bailey	
15	Tony Saban		Tony Saban	
16	Mike Nicholls		Mike Nicholls	
17	Bill Roberts		Bill Roberts	
18	Andrew Hulme		Andrew Hulme	
19	Peter Bass		Peter Bass	
20	Lawrence Bailey		Lawrence Bailey	
21	Peter Gillman	**Peter Gillman**		
22	John Riseborough		John Riseborough	
23	Alasdair MacGillivray		Alasdair MacGillivray	
24	Charles Olley	**Charles Olley**		
25	Peter Crouch		Peter Crouch	
26	David Robinson		David Robinson	
27	Rodney Wolverson		Rodney Wolverson	
28	Richard Day	**Richard Day**		
29	Colin Long		Colin Long	
30	Simon Brook		Simon Brook	

(continued)

	Current	Former	Deceased
31 Steve Everall		Steve Everall	
32 Paul Martin		Paul Martin	
33 Nick Pollington	**Nick Pollington**		
34 Graham Bradley		Graham Bradley	
35 Nick Mayhew	**Nick Mayhew**		
36 Martin Clapson	**Martin Clapson**		
37 Peter Cadle		Peter Cadle	
38 Howard Sears	**Howard Sears**		
39 Tony Everitt		Tony Everitt	
40 Richard Setchell		Richard Setchell	
41 Trevor Smith	**Trevor Smith**		
42 Andrew Youles		Andrew Youles	
43 Paul Cullen	**Paul Cullen**		
44 Paul Dearsley	**Paul Dearsley**		
45 Tony Sanderson	**Tony Sanderson**		
46 James King	**James King**		
47 Ian Coombes			Ian Coombes
48 Richard Vass	**Richard Vass**		
49 Daren Moore	**Daren Moore**		
50 Iain Robertson		Iain Robertson	
51 Fenella Martin-Redman		Fenella Martin-Redman	
52 Gary Miller	**Gary Miller**		
53 Simon Blake	**Simon Blake**		
54 Colin Pickard		Colin Pickard	
55 Aaron Widdows	**Aaron Widdows**		
56 Matt Coward	**Matt Coward**		
57 John Warren	**John Warren**		
58 Jitu Shah	**Jitu Shah**		
59 Tony Pennison	**Tony Pennison**		
60 Helena Wilkinson	**Helena Wilkinson**		

Appendix 2

Every company receives misspelt names and addresses. Here are some of Price Bailey's more amusing ones:

```
PRINCE BAILEY
CAUSEWAY HOUSE
1 DANE STREET
BISHOP'S STORTFORD
HERTS CM23 3BT
```

```
St. Price Esq FCA.,
Messrs. Price Bailey & Partners
The Guild House
Water Lane
BISHOP'S STORTFORD
Herts
```

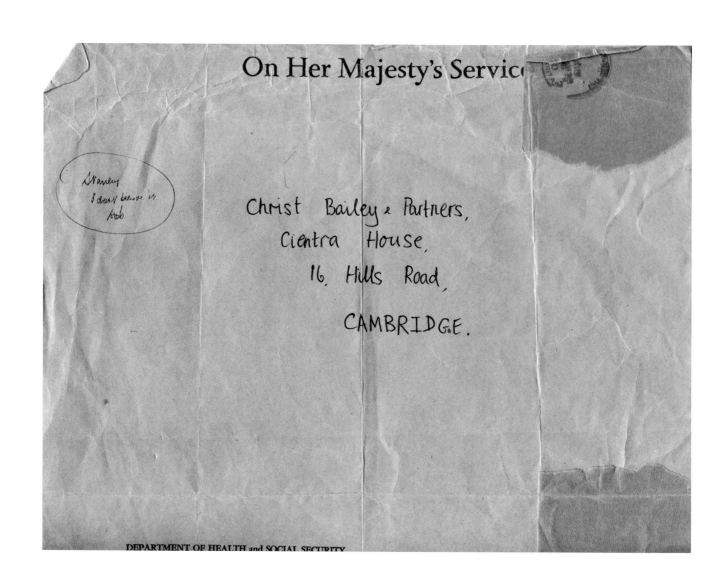

On Her Majesty's Service

Stanley
I don't believe it
Bob

Christ Bailey & Partners,
Cientra House,
16, Hills Road,

CAMBRIDGE.

DEPARTMENT OF HEALTH and SOCIAL SECURITY

Index

(Entries in *italics* refer to photographs of individuals)